ROUTLEDGE LIBRARY EDITIONS:
ETHICS

Volume 8

THE CONCEPT OF MORALITY

THE CONCEPT OF MORALITY

PRATIMA BOWES

Routledge
Taylor & Francis Group

LONDON AND NEW YORK

First published in 1959 by George Allen & Unwin Ltd

This edition first published in 2021
by Routledge
2 Park Square, Milton Park, Abingdon, Oxon OX14 4RN

and by Routledge
52 Vanderbilt Avenue, New York, NY 10017

Routledge is an imprint of the Taylor & Francis Group, an informa business

© 1959 Pratima Bowes

British Library Cataloguing in Publication Data
A catalogue record for this book is available from the British Library

ISBN: 978-0-367-85624-3 (Set)
ISBN: 978-1-00-305260-9 (Set) (ebk)
ISBN: 978-0-367-90062-5 (Volume 8) (hbk)
ISBN: 978-1-00-302224-4 (Volume 8) (ebk)

Publisher's Note
The publisher has gone to great lengths to ensure the quality of this reprint but points out that some imperfections in the original copies may be apparent.

Disclaimer
The publisher has made every effort to trace copyright holders and would welcome correspondence from those they have been unable to trace.

The Concept

of

Morality

PRATIMA BOWES

Ruskin House

GEORGE ALLEN & UNWIN LTD

MUSEUM STREET LONDON

*Printed in Great Britain
in 12 point Bembo type
by Purnell and Sons Ltd
Paulton (Somerset) and London*

ACKNOWLEDGMENTS

This book is, with minor alterations, an abridged version of the Ph.D. Thesis, *The Concept of Morality*, which I submitted to the University of London in 1955. The work was done under Prof. H. B. Acton of Bedford College and it took shape through my trying to cope with Prof. Acton's criticisms, some of which were very destructive. It is true to say that had there not been these criticisms I would never have gained whatever degree of clarity of thought and expression I have been able to achieve in these pages. For this I am deeply grateful to Prof. Acton. I shall not mention my indebtedness to any other philosopher by name, for there is scarcely a book on Ethics, ancient or modern, which I have not read with profit. I am greatly indebted to my mother-in-law, Mrs H. Bowes, who made it possible for me to study by offering to look after my young daughter, and to my husband, Mr. S Bowes, for all the assistance and encouragement he gave me.

PRATIMA BOWES

Shri Shikshayatan College
Calcutta
1958

CONTENTS

I shall first of all try to state as clearly as I can the scope and objectives of this work. An enquiry is limited by the questions that one selects for consideration out of the many that may be asked on the problem at hand; and it is important for us to note what precisely are the questions to which answers are being sought.

Some of the important issues discussed in moral philosophy in recent years are the following: (*a*) Is a philosophical treatment of Ethics at all possible or is it metaphysical in the derogatory sense of the term? (*b*) Are philosophical questions in morals questions of language or are there genuine moral questions of a non-linguistic character? (*c*) Is Ethics a theoretical study concerned with the knowledge of objective facts or is it concerned merely with our attitudes, decisions and commands and consequently is not a matter of knowledge at all? (*d*) If we admit that there are facts to be theoretically approached in Ethics, how do we come to know them—can we say we know them by intuition? (*e*) Has reason a place in Ethics? If it has, how far can it go? (*f*) Can we claim that a moral principle like 'the truth ought to be told' is self-evident, arguing at the same time that the nature of moral reasoning is deductive? For this would mean that we must speak the truth whenever the question of speaking the truth or otherwise is relevant. And this contradicts our conviction that there may arise situations in which it will be morally better not to tell the truth. It is with these questions that this enquiry is concerned.

To foretell the general line that my attempt to answer these questions will take. I believe that general moral concepts like 'ought', 'good' and 'right' embody conceptions of standards in accordance with which particular moral judgments proceed (or they ought to proceed) and these may in some sense become objects of theoretical understanding and knowledge—and hence to be treated as facts in some context of a moral nature—in an ethical enquiry that is philosophical in character. Preliminary to developing my position as to what these concepts stand for, I shall examine some of the theories which suggest that the function of ethical philosophy is something quite other than what traditional philosophers believed it to be, namely to ask questions like 'What is good?' and 'What is justice?' I do not think that the traditional questions were entirely on the wrong track (I do not say this is the only type of philosophical questions that one may ask in Ethics), although I would say that traditional philosophers did not always make clear the contexts of their enquiries which determined the questions they asked, nor did they always state the questions in unambiguous language. And this perhaps helps to create confusions as to what they were doing.

My enquiry in its positive aspect is analytic, its object being to clarify the implications of conceptions which we use when we evaluate aspects of our experience from a distinctive point of view, namely that of morality. (It therefore takes the legitimacy of the moral point of view for granted.) What I have said so far may suggest that moral terms have a precise significance in usage which they clearly have not; indeed, usage allows the application of these terms in more than one way. Nevertheless, I believe that these terms have some sort of an identifiable reference where they are used *consistently* within a characteristic way of looking at things, which, it is important to note, is believed to be an impersonal way. It will be one of my tasks here to expound what this characteristic point of view is.

It will perhaps be better—to avoid possible misunderstandings —to emphasize at the outset that I do not advocate that our particular moral judgments about our duties in specific situations of life, about a person's character or conduct, about an existing state of affairs and so on, are of the nature of empirically verifiable statements or that it is possible for us to obtain infallible particular judgments in such matters. Again, even though I have talked about standards of moral judgments, these standards are not of the nature of tests, as the term 'test' will be understood in a scientific context, by applying which particular judgments may immediately be labelled as true or false. Rather, I believe that the immense complexity of human nature and situations, relations and states of affairs—issues which we judge morally—renders the vast majority of our particular moral judgments only more or less probable. I shall no doubt use in this enquiry the terms 'intuition' and 'self-evident', but it is only general moral standards which are intuitively grasped to be self-evident, and not particular moral judgments which deal with specific issues of a particular character. I quite realize that what worries people is the variety of moral opinions and judgments, often on the same issue, and they turn to philosophy in the hope of obtaining a sort of yardstick by which to measure their validity. No such thing, however, can be got out of the philosophical bag and people (strangely enough, some philosophers too) are apt to lose interest in a book of Ethics which tells them that even though terms like 'objectivity', 'validity' and 'knowledge' are applicable in the moral sphere, we have no ready-made test by which the claim of a partcular moral judgment to be tenable may be decided. I am afraid this book has little to offer people who would like a book of Ethics to take over the very difficult task of having to make moral decisions from their hands by settling their moral conflicts and disputes automatically in terms of set formulas. A book of this kind can only help to clear some of the confusions and misunderstandings that stand in the way of a rational use of moral concepts. Any contribution it makes towards solving practical moral problems can thus only be very indirect, although it is true that an enquiry into general concepts is initiated through difficulties and confusions that are felt in practical contexts. When all is said and done, the responsibility for thinking out moral solutions—whenever such solutions are to be found—lies with the moral agent. So does the responsibility to decide to act in a particular way in a complex situation. Yet a clearer understanding of ethical concepts—their use or what they stand for—may help one in one's deliberation by giving it a certain direction. This may not be much in a world where problems of ever-increasing complexity are continually being pushed forward in our way. Yet for one who is really confused as to what to make of moral questions in the face of conflicting opinions about the nature of morals, this sort of enquiry might be of some use.

The complexity of moral issues not only makes our particular judgments fallible, it makes some of our moral disputes irresolvable, particularly at a certain stage of deliberation, as there are only certain guiding principles (standards) of ethical thinking but no ready-made tests by applying which an agreement may be forced. Principles may guide our thinking towards a certain direction; they cannot, as moral problems go, absolutely determine the course or the conclusion of a process of deliberation. It is this irresolvability that has led some moral philosophers to deny that moral discourse is in any way a matter of rational understanding. It is my wish to suggest that we can recognize the irresolvable character of some particular moral disputes and yet say that there is such a thing as 'rational understanding of morals'. To say this is to say that moral discourse has (or ought to have) a certain general character, the framework of which can be rationally approached and understood. Even to have gained this point is a definite advantage when we weigh it against the implications of theories which claim that moral judgments are purely matters of emotions, attitudes, commands and so on. Of course, at bottom there will be little difference between philosophers who put forward these theories and those who believe in morals in the old sense; for these theories are so many recommendations to use certain terms rather than others in describing what are usually known as moral judgments, considering that they differ in some important ways from what are usually known as scientific judgments. Yet, it seems to me that a confusion between particular moral judgments and general moral standards is concealed in the denial of the use of terms like 'objectivity' and 'validity' in the moral sphere, but this is a very important distinction to grasp and remember. For a particular dispute may involve such complexity that the application of general standards may not help us to arrive at any definite conclusion. Yet such standards may, with respect to a different type of issue, not only guide us to a certain direction but also thereby lead us to a definite conclusion which is rationally more acceptable than another which we may have to accept if we did not apply these standards. In any case, the belief that one may be right or wrong in moral matters or that morality is in some sense objective is widely prevalent—and not only amongst some misguided philosophers. Not that a belief generally held cannot be wrong, but it is worth one's while to try to find out what, if anything, lies behind such a belief which may render the holding of it justified. For a belief ought to be discarded and a new way of talking necessitated by such discarding introduced only when there is no justification for continuing in it. I wish to say that this belief is justified if it is taken to refer to the nature of moral standards in accordance with which particular judgments ought to proceed and not directly to particular judgments themselves. Merely to say that moral judgments are not right or wrong or that they have no objective reference is to obscure the fact that there are certain appropriate and rationally approachable standards of assessment in moral matters, whatever the difficulties and outcome of applying these to any particular case. In case of a moral dispute we can only try to defend our own judgment (a defence which will have any hope of hearing from other people) by appealing to a standard objectively acceptable as valid in this sphere by all concerned and not by saying that, since there is no test of truth here, our own judgment has as much claim to acceptance as that of the opponent. Such are my justifications for embarking on a work which, I am aware, is somewhat old-fashioned.

CHAPTER I

The Nature of Philosophy of Ethics

PART I. IS PHILOSOPHY OF ETHICS POSSIBLE?

The view that what goes by the name of Philosophy of Ethics is a confusion caused by lack of understanding of the use of ethical terms has recently become popular. Philosophy of Ethics, it is maintained, should properly be meta-ethics, i.e. an enquiry into the logic and language of ethical terms. The only objection I have to this recommendation is that it suggests that an enquiry into the logic and language of ethical terms is purely a linguistic enquiry and not, as I believe, into what may be called 'moral facts or characteristics' as well.

C. L. Stevenson in his *Ethics and Language* draws a distinction between normative and philosophical ethics and claims that only the former is legitimate. If I understand him all right the distinction is this. Normative ethics is what we are all concerned with when we make our ordinary value judgments on people's conduct and character and also on existing states of affairs. Philosophical ethics, according to Stevenson, is based on the mistaken idea that there are certain intrinsic and ultimate ends of conduct which exist quite independently of any matters of fact. As Stevenson may be taken to be representative of the school of thought which denies philosophical ethics its pride of place, we may consider his arguments against it somewhat in detail.

Talking about philosophical ethics, he says that questions of value occur only in connection with questions of fact, and what are called intrinsic ends cannot exist without some means being adopted to bring them into existence. It is therefore futile to treat values as if they exist on their own independently of any fact and as if one could discuss these values quite apart from a factual context. Again, it is useless to suppose that a discussion about intrinsic ends can be profitable quite apart from a context in which the question of adopting some means or other to bring them into existence is relevant. If values do not exist except in so far as facts are considered valuable and if intrinsic ends do not exist except through the instrumentality of means, then questions about intrinsic value cannot constitute an independent study as philosophical moralists thought they can. It is the statesmen, psychologists, social scientists, etc., who pass normative judgments about the particular objects of their concern—people who are engaged in discussing not what is desirable as an end for its own sake but the relationship between certain states of affairs and certain courses of human actions which lead to such states—who are properly engaged on questions of value. And the sort of questions they ask is the only sort of value questions that it is important for us to ask.

Now one would entirely agree with Stevenson that values do not exist except in the context of facts, and that in actual life there are not two sets of questions—questions about values and intrinsic ends to be dealt with by specialists (philosophical moralists) and questions of facts and means to be asked by statesmen, social scientists, etc. One would also agree that it is not the case that if and when the latter group of people wish to decide upon objectives they should consult the specialists in value. Nevertheless, I do not agree that questions about intrinsic ends cannot form an independent study or that philosophical moralists, who in a certain sense divorce questions of fact and means from questions of value and ends, do not ask questions as significant for human purposes as the questions asked by statesmen, etc., who are concerned with directly existing facts and with means to bring about changes believed to be preferable to states of affairs actually existing. I have tried to indicate in my discussions on the concepts of 'good' and 'right' how the questions of intrinsic ends can become objects of an independent study. Here I shall indicate very briefly what I conceive a philosophical treatment of Ethics to be and in what sense philosophical moralists are justified in divorcing the questions of ends and values from questions of means and facts.

Value questions, as Stevenson says, arise only in factual contexts. When statesmen are engaged in dealing with international political problems in the course of which they deliberate whether they should go to war to solve a dispute or whether they should meet the opponent half-way (speaking figuratively) and settle the issue peacefully they are engaged in settling questions of value. Let us suppose that the statesmen engaged in a conflict between two governments are X and Y and the issue is Z, and naturally it is highly complex. That is to say, it has not got a simple, clearcut, precise nature that can be got hold of by using our senses and it itself is composed of different issues of a less general kind or has many aspects.[1] Now both the statesmen X and Y are concerned with Z but with different aspects of it or with Z as looked at from different points of view, and let us suppose that these are P and Q. P and Q themselves are systems of things rather than particular things, and as systems are in some ways opposed to one another. X upholds P and opposes Q, while Y does the reverse. Let us suppose, further, that they then pass the value judgments 'P is so much better than Q that one is justified in going to war in order to have P instead of Q' and 'Q is so much, etc.'.

Now R, who is an ordinary citizen in either of the countries the governments of which are in opposition, might find that his own reactions to the matter are somewhat different. He might feel that neither P nor Q is thoroughly good or thoroughly bad and it is not at all obvious to him that P is so much better than Q that one is justified in starting a war that has immeasurable powers of destruction in order that P may exist as against Q or vice versa. As some people say that P is good and Q bad and others make the opposite judgment, R feels that he needs a standard acceptable to all reasonable people by which to decide— if such a decision is at all possible. The issue is so important for so many people that he feels that it ought not to be decided in such

[1] For instance if the issue is human freedom one could discern various aspects of the problem and talk about freedom of speech and political opinion, economic freedom or basic security and a standard of life for the mass of population which is in keeping with the wealth of the country, freedom or opportunity to exercise genuine choice in selecting one's career in accordance with one's capabilities and so on.

a way as inflicts a lot of suffering on them—purely on grounds of personal preference.

R might find in the course of deliberation that P appears good as against Q because of its aspects a, b, c, etc., the comparable ones in Q being i, j, k; and Q appears good as against P because of its aspects e, f, g, etc., the comparable ones in P being m, n, o. The aspects i, j, k, etc., in Q are such that their existence definitely makes it difficult and in certain cases even impossible for some individual human beings to fulfil some of their deeply felt needs, as a result of which they cannot develop themselves in their own ways or live their own lives as they would like to, whereas the existence of a, b, c does not mean this for the same group of people. Again, the aspects m, n, o are such that their presence means the continuation of an injustice of a certain kind to some people, whereas the presence of aspects e, f, g does not mean this. When X says 'P is good' he is possibly talking about the aspects a, b, c, etc., in it, and the standard by which he is judging such things to be good is the conception 'opportunity for people to develop and live in their own ways'. When Y says 'Q is good' he is possibly talking about the aspects e, f, g in it, and the standard by which he is judging such things to be good is the conception of 'justice'. These conceptions are acceptable as standards of evaluation because the conceptions which oppose them like 'lack of opportunity for people to develop and live in their own ways' and 'lack of justice' cannot, from the very nature of the case, be appealed to by reasonable people to support the worthwhileness of what they value. That is to say, these concepts are such that they show themselves to be reasonable courts of appeal in certain contexts of evaluation, while the opposite conceptions show themselves to be unreasonable. The man may further reflect on the question, why is it that we accept these conceptions as standards and not the conceptions which oppose them, and find that these conceptions are consistent with the possibility of the happiness of human beings as individuals, while the conceptions which oppose these are not. And he further finds that it is reasonable, from the very nature of the case, to prefer human happiness to unhappiness, while it is unreasonable to do the opposite.

R thus finds that there are certain conceptions of standards by appealing to which the worthwhileness of certain things valued may be supported and this support may be expected to be satisfactory to people who will take up a reasonable attitude towards the question. That is to say, these standards have been conceived in such a way that an appeal to these rather than to their opposites is reasonable and this appeal does not need the support of arguments to show that it is reasonable. It is then the case that the notions of certain self-justified standards or ends are actually implied in our evaluation of human affairs when we believe that our evaluation stands for something over and above personal preference, i.e. when we believe that if people are reasonable they will accept the worthwhileness of what we are valuing.

When R has come to have a fuller understanding of the conceptions that have been involved as the standards of evaluation of the states of affairs P and Q he might find that the actual judgments passed on P and Q are not fully satisfactory from the point of view of morality. Although aspects *a*, *b*, *c*, etc., of P are in accordance with a self-evident standard and in that sense good, there are certain other aspects of P, namely *m*, *n*, *o*, which do not satisfy another self-evident standard as well as the aspects *e*, *f*, *g* of Q do. Therefore the judgment 'P is good' is not tenable as a value judgment if it is meant to be an unqualified judgment to the effect that P is good through and through and not merely that P is good in so far as P involves *a*, *b*, *c*, etc. A similar remark holds of Q. R might still find that it is possible to say that P is on the whole better than Q and vice versa if it is at all possible to find that the one or the other leaves greater scope for the happiness of human beings as individuals when considered in the totality of their aspects. But he finds that the judgment 'P is so much better than Q that one is justified in going to war so that one may have P instead of Q'[1], or vice versa, is untenable as a value judgment because it is inconsistent with the requirements of human happiness as individuals. War as a method of solving disputes is one matter when it injures a restricted group of people

---

[1] The actual judgments passed are much more complex. I have taken a simplified case for the sake of argument.

directly involved in fighting, it is quite another when the lives
and possessions of a large number of people are involved who are
neither responsible in any way for creating tension nor are personally interested in solving the dispute to such a degree that
they do not any longer consider their lives and possessions to be
valuable. For in the latter case starting a war means forcing a lot
of people to be extremely unhappy when the unhappiness involved is such that the people concerned neither desire nor
deserve it. Reflections on the meaning of ethical terms—when
these terms are used in a judgment which the evaluator believes
to stand for something more than an expression of personal
opinion—then may actually lead us to consider some value
judgments passed to be unsatisfactory or not wholly tenable, in
so far as these judgments claim to be objective.

Philosophical ethics has to do with our thinking about ethical
issues and with the satisfactory or unsatisfactory use of ethical
terms in a value context which is accepted by the disputants to
be in some sense objective (otherwise there can hardly be any
argument and the matter would end with the voicing of personal
preferences). It is then concerned with the clarification of the
meaning of ethical terms in one sense and with intrinsic ends or
self-justified standards of value in another, for unless conceptions
of such standards are involved in the use of ethical terms the
value context is not such that a judgment which is more than an
expression of a personal preference can be passed. It is concerned
with the clarification of the meaning of ethical terms in this
sense. Ethical judgments use such terms of evaluation as 'right'
and 'good'. Some ethical judgments, at any rate, claim to be more
than expressions of personal attitudes and preferences inasmuch
as people making such judgments believe that others would find
them acceptable if they looked at them from a value point of
view that is rational. Now reasonable people may be expected to
accept these judgments only if such judgments are in accordance
with conceptions of standards that they will find acceptable
because of their being what they are. In normative judgments of
the sort that we are discussing, then, the terms 'right' and 'good'
may be expected to involve certain self-justified standards of

value or, which is the same thing, to be consistent with conceptions of intrinsic ends. Philosophical ethics may profitably enquire what these self-justifying standards (and their implications) are that are involved in the use of the terms like 'right' and 'good' in ordinary normative discourse when that discourse is held consistently within a characteristic point of view and when it is presumed to be based on something more than personal preference. To do this is, in a sense, to explicate or analyse the meaning of these terms. And this analysis can be a guide in our approach to some of the actual uses that are made of such terms. For instance, if we say that a part of the meaning of the ethical term 'good'—when this term is used consistently within a characteristic point of view—is that whatever is referred to by that term may be supposed to be consistent with the conception of greatest good (a state of affairs in which it is possible for everyone concerned to be as happy as it is in his nature to be), then a particular use of the ethical term 'good' (or 'better') as in 'it will be better to go to war for P than not to have P' may be shown to be ethically untenable, if there is reason to think that the war in question will cause more unhappiness to human beings as individuals than the state of affairs lacking in P. Or again, take another ethical term 'justice' which stands for a self-justifying standard generally believed to be good. If we define justice as a state of affairs in which nobody is treated prejudicially or preferentially in respect of fulfilment of his felt needs—and we can do so if we find that this is how this term is used in ordinary normative discourse when it is used consistently—then the use of the term 'just' as in 'a society in which people do their duties belonging to their stations in life is just' may be shown to be ethically untenable. But this analysis of the meaning of ethical terms is at the same time an enquiry into intrinsic ends or self-justifying standards. For philosophical ethics does not just discuss the different senses in which ethical terms are actually used but tries to discern that particular meaning, out of all that are current in usage, which can be consistently applied from a characteristic point of view; and such consistent use of a value term can only be understood with reference to the conception of a standard that does not need any further support of arguments to show that it is acceptable.

Philosophical ethics then divorces the conceptions of ends for a specialized study from the questions of means, i.e. it discusses what is involved in the conception of the self-justifying end called 'justice' without discussing how justice in some particular sphere or other can be brought about. (I do not say that a philosopher cannot do this as well.) But the conception of the end called 'justice' with which it is legitimately concerned is not a conception that is spun out of a philosopher's head, rather it is a conception that is found by the philosopher to be implicit in the undertaking of certain means by some people to bring about certain changes in the existing states of affairs, as also in some actual normative discourse. Only, the philosopher endeavours to choose a meaning that can be consistently employed within a certain characteristic context of discourse.

The justification of a philosophical treatment of Ethics then lies in this. It is not that the statesmen, social scientists and the like should learn what things are intrinsically good from the philosophers, for they themselves are not lacking in the ideas of ends. On the contrary, they are concerned with the question of means only because they have ends to realize. But ethical terms stand for conceptions that are abstract and complex in nature and it is not unlikely that in a normative discourse they are sometimes used inconsistently, i.e. the same term is used to imply different things not consistent with one another in different judgments put forward in the same context of discourse. A philosopher's study of the implications of an ethical term may here be of use by helping the argument to be consistent and to the point. The philosophers do not contribute to the laymen the conceptions of intrinsic ends, for they themselves arrive at the ideas of these ends in course of reflecting on some of the conduct, character, emotions, thoughts, and aspirations of people, including non-philosophers. Their contribution—supposing that they succeed in contributing anything—lies in explicating the consistent implications of these ends when the ideas of these ends are used from a characteristic point of view.

If philosophical ethics is conceived in the manner indicated above, then some of the damaging criticisms that Stevenson offers against philosophical ethics, which he calls the 'specialist's conception of ethics', will not affect our position. One of his main criticisms is that philosophical ethics requires that we should derive moral conclusions about matters of fact by way of deduction from self-evident premises with which only philosophical moralists, the specialists in value, have any concern.

But I do not think that a philosophical moralist is necessarily committed to the opinion that moral arguments are deductive. He might say that instead of starting with a general proposition that something or other is intrinsically good we actually start with the opinion that something or other in particular is good or bad and when such opinion is questioned we advance general considerations of the nature of standards on which our valuation can find a support in the eyes of others, or again we might be faced with a situation which we find to be unsatisfactory in some ways but do not know at a glance what exactly is bad or wrong about it or how it should be changed. This is a situation which leads us on to a process of ethical deliberation. In order that our deliberation may proceed we shall have to find why it is that we find the situation unsatisfactory or by what standard we are judging it to be so. Then it becomes possible for us to see in greater detail what exactly are the features in the situation which are inconsistent with the conception of the standard. And it is then that we proceed to think of means by which changes can be effected, and some of the proposed means may appear to be inconsistent—under a given set of circumstances—with general conceptions of standards that we accept, while others may not. As general conceptions are formed out of reflection on particular happenings it is vital for a philosopher to be acquainted with particulars of experience even though his special concern may be with general conceptions and not with any happening in particular. He cannot be, as Stevenson puts it, pardonably ignorant of the causes of M's and N's, for they do have something to do with the understanding of intrinsic values. But if M's and N's are facts that belong specially to, say, sociology, he cannot be expected to have as expert or as detailed a knowledge of them as a sociologist. It is enough for him to know them as well as is necessary to see their general value implications. If the actual argument runs as follows: X is good because (supposing that this contention is questioned or needs support in some ways) it leads to a preponderance of M's over N's and M is a sort of thing that is worthwhile for its own sake in human affairs, then what is involved is not a division of labour, as Stevenson alleges, between people who will collect by means of logic and scientific method the second premise of the argument and the philosophers who will supply the first, but a reflective or philosophical understanding (i.e. an understanding that is conscious of the consistent implications of what is being said) of that part of the argument, 'X leads to a preponderance of M's and M is the sort of thing that is worthwhile for its own sake in human affairs', on the part of those who will argue that X is good or contest it. Such understanding may already be there, or it may become fuller or more mature by listening to what the philosophers have to say— philosophers who have made a special study of the matter, and reflected on the general implications of particular acts of evaluation when such evaluations are made from a consistent and characteristic point of view.

Stevenson wants us to replace philosophical ethics by normative ethics. As far as I can make out, normative questions are like this. 'Should or should there not be unemployment benefit in the country X?', 'Is caste or class distinctions in the society X a state of affairs that can be supported from an ethical point of view?', 'Should people in general have more leisure in society X than they at present enjoy?' and so on. I quite agree that the asking of such questions is important and that philosophers can be profitably engaged in exploring them. But I would add that something more remains to be done and this is an analysis of the value conceptions which act as standards of judgments in normative and practical questions of the type Stevenson asks. It is the task of philosophical ethics to undertake such an analysis.

PART 2. ARE ETHICAL QUESTIONS QUESTIONS OF LANGUAGE?

Let us now see what are the sorts of things that are claimed by saying that an ethical question is a question of language. 'Ethics,' says Hare in the preface to his book *The Language of Morals*, 'as I conceive it, is the logical study of the language of morals.' This, of course, does not rule out the possibility of moral problems being factual. It might mean that the best approach to the understanding of facts Ethics deals with is through a logical analysis of terms used in morals. For language is logical in so far as the terms employed successfully convey the distinctive differences and similarities between relevant aspects of our experience; so it is possible to understand the characteristics of a specific kind of facts through an understanding of the logic of the terms used to convey their nature. Yet the logical analysis Hare carries out of such ethical terms as 'right', 'ought' and 'good' does not bring us any nearer to what are morally right and good. Nor—if what is right or good has such a specifically individual character that a general formulation of it independently of the context to which it belongs is impossible—does it offer us a suitable criterion by which what is of moral value can be distinguished from what is not. The only criterion Hare suggests is that moral value concerns conduct about which we get easily stirred up or which concerns man as man, but this is much too vague. We get stirred up, says Hare, if Mrs Smith does not pay her fare on the railways because we might ourselves be travelling. But it is quite possible that a person who uses the railways almost every day gets stirred up only because Mrs Smith is caught, and that he would not be in the least disturbed if Mrs Smith's action, which he knows of, passed unnoticed by the railway authorities. He might even contemplate following her example. But the major part of Hare's analysis is logical in the sense that it concerns the language of morals and not in the sense that it concerns the facts such language deals with. Here I shall attempt to state very briefly what Hare has to say about ethical terms. If a sentence uses the term 'right' it really is an imperative sentence and not an indicative one. A moral command to do something cannot be derived from facts but presupposes an imperative sentence whose function is prescriptive (i.e. it tells us to do something) rather than descriptive (which tells us that something is the case). The inference involved in a moral decision is as rigorous as any other inference, only with this difference: that it contains an irreducible prescriptive element as its premise. The meaning of the term 'good' is both evaluative and descriptive, but in morals it is the evaluative sense that is primary. However, evaluation is nothing peculiar to morals as it is present in all value judgments, instrumental or intrinsic. Its evaluative meaning lies in this, that it commends something to our choice. 'X is good' means X is the sort of man we should choose to become, just as 'this is a good chronometer' means this is the chronometer or sort of chronometer we should choose if we were going to buy one. And we understand the meaning of these sentences independently of any criteria of goodness that there may be. Similarly the term 'ought' has a descriptive force but its primary function is to prescribe or advise or instruct; and this function can be fulfilled when no information is being conveyed. It is an answer to the question 'What shall I do?'.

There is much more in this book, of course, that is instructive and important. What is relevant for my purposes here is to note that Hare's analysis is, in the main, concerned not so much with the facts of morals as with the language of morals. Now, it is not my intention to suggest that an inquiry into the language of morals is not profitable, nor am I concerned with the details of the analysis itself. All I wish to say is that there are problems of morals over and above the problems that are peculiar to the language of morals, and if one has tackled the latter one has not necessarily tackled the former as well. But it does not appear that Hare has made a distinction between these two different sorts of problems; rather he may be taken to suggest that a discussion of the questions connected with the language of morals means a discussion of the problems of morals itself.

Some philosophers, even though they do not belong to the linguistic school of thought, believe that questions like 'What is justice?' traditionally asked by the body of enquiry called

'Ethics' are verbal questions. 'What do we really mean when we speak of "justice"?' asks Popper. 'I do not think that verbal questions of this kind are particularly important, or that it is possible to give a definite reply to them, since such terms are always used in various senses.'[1]

Now, there is a sense in which some questions in Ethics are verbal. Suppose the question is, 'Is it just that a person born into a low caste should not be allowed to enter a temple where the higher castes worship God?' The answer may be 'yes' or 'no'. Those who would say 'yes' would perhaps define justice as a state of affairs where people keep to the rights and duties belonging to their stations in life so that the harmony of the social structure is not disturbed. If a social structure in its entirety is such that it needs an untouchable caste, then it is just, according to this conception, that untouchables should not demand the same rights as others. If, on the other hand, by a just[2] state of affairs we mean one where every individual is treated as potentially equal to every other in respect of fulfilment of needs—provided that such needs do not necessarily interfere with the needs of others which we may consider to be legitimate under the circumstances—and any actual difference made is based on the merits and capabilities of the individuals concerned, then the answer is 'no'. We all need the respect and recognition of our fellow individuals. This need is frustrated if some people are treated as inferior to others for no other reason than the fact that they are born in a family the status of which in the structure of the society is already fixed as low independently of any considerations of the merits and capabilities of its members. The question we have asked can be considered to be verbal in so far as the answer follows naturally from the definition of justice involved. But is there any reason why we should accept both these definitions as equally satisfactory? To say that because the term 'justice' is used in various senses, all we are entitled to do is to make it clear what amongst the various possible senses we are adopting for the purposes of discussion and

---

[1] *The Open Society*, vol. i, p. 77.

[2] This conception does not describe any actually existing state of affairs but we consider existing states of affairs as more or less just according as they satisfy its requirements.

not judge in what sense it ought to be used, is to be guilty of a sort of naturalism.

The question 'What is justice?' is verbal, says Popper. Nevertheless he offers us what he considers to be the essential requirements of it. '... (a) an equal distribution of the burden of citizenship, i.e. of those limitations of freedom which are necessary in social life; (b) equal treatment of the citizens before the law, provided, of course, that (c) the laws themselves neither favour nor disfavour individual citizens or groups or classes; (d) impartiality of the courts of justice; and (e) an equal share in the advantages (and not only in the burden) which their membership of the state may offer to the citizen.'[1] These, of course, are not provided for in the definition that Plato gives of 'justice' in *The Republic* and as a result he comes under severe criticism in *The Open Society* and is even blamed for his unjust intentions. If this is a verbal question it is difficult to see how Popper is justified in being so hard on Plato, since presumably people are entitled to differ on questions that are verbal (the reason why they are called verbal), so long as they make it clear how they are using a term. It may, of course, be said that Popper considers the verbal question to be unimportant, not the moral one. But if Plato is engaged in *The Republic* with the question of defining 'justice' and if the question of defining 'justice' is purely a verbal question, then it is possible, theoretically at any rate, that Plato's moral views are not unacceptable no matter how he defines 'justice'. If this does not sound plausible, then perhaps the confusion is caused by the theory that the question of definition is purely a verbal question (no doubt there is a verbal question involved as well in the question of definition) and not a question of adequate characterization of certain facts as well.

There is another possible sense in which this question may be said to be verbal. Individual human personalities are very complex psychophysical organisms and their needs and capabilities are of various kinds and degrees; so is a society with its peculiar configuration manifested in its diverse but inter-related institutions. It is possible that even if we agree on a definition of justice, which

[1] *The Open Society*, vol. i, p. 77.

is necessarily very general and formal, we may be unable to deduce from it any definite conclusion regarding a particular society. An inference concerning the just character of a society may run as follows:

> The state of affairs P Q R is just.
> > (and this is agreed)
> The society X exhibits P Q R.
> The society X is just.

The minor premise in a syllogism stands for some observed fact. But it is the minor premise in this particular case, that society X exhibits P Q R that will be the occasion of most serious disagreement. One of the requirements of justice mentioned by Popper is that laws should show neither favour nor disfavour towards individual citizens or groups or classes. Now the very conception of a law (in the legal sense) implies that its transgressors should be punished according to some definite standard no matter who they are. In most societies there is a law against stealing. Suppose that a man in a highly industrialized society is unemployed for some time and some of his essential needs are frustrated over a period of time due to lack of money. This man steals, is brought before the court and is punished. Another man, who holds a highly paid job, would, of course, receive the same punishment if he commits the same offence. Do the laws in this society show neither favour nor disfavour towards individual citizens, groups or classes? Some may say 'yes' and others 'no'. Those who would say 'no' may do so because the particular laws that exist are necessary for the harmonious working of any society and these laws are administered with strict impartiality. Those who would say 'yes' may do so because they believe that the laws of an economically developed society should guarantee employment, and a wage adequate for maintaining a standard of life compatible with the economic potentialities of the society in question, to every able and willing individual. If such laws are non-existent, then it cannot be said that the laws show neither favour nor disfavour. Nor does the disagreement end here. The questions 'What are the economic potentialities of this society?' and 'What sort of standard of life is decent in this society considering that its economic potentialities are of such and such character?' are not easy to solve and require specialized knowledge for their discussion. Moreover, they give rise to further questions in the process of our trying to solve them.

It is thus evident that the just character or otherwise of a particular society cannot be arrived at by a process of simple deduction from the definition of justice. And substantially the same disagreement may remain about some vital factual questions like 'Do the laws favour or disfavour any individual group or class in this society?' or 'Do people in this society enjoy a standard of life compatible with its economic potentialities?' no matter how we define justice. It may therefore be felt that the question of definition of justice is a verbal question and not one that concerns matters of fact. But those who feel this way are really demanding the impossible. How can a definition of justice tell us what the economic possibilities of a particular society are? If we want an answer to this question, supposing this question can be answered, we shall have to find out a lot of things about those specific kinds of facts which are technically known as economic.

It may now be asked how exactly is the question of defining 'justice' a factual question. I shall merely touch upon it here as the question will be dealt with in greater detail in the next chapter. Let us take a moral judgment 'the state of affairs X is just'. X is here the thing judged, so it may be said to constitute the content of this judgment. It is not enough, in order that we may be in a position to pass this judgment, for us to know about X. We must also have some idea what is meant by the term 'just' or 'justice'. When we have this idea we see that many other social institutions and human relations (actual or possible) may be looked upon as just or unjust according as they do or do not satisfy the requirements of this idea. The idea of justice is then a standard in accordance with which the moral value of certain sorts of things is judged. It may then be called the form of the value judgment 'X is just' inasmuch as the conception of justice embodies a characteristic way of looking at whatever is X.[1] Now the concept of justice is formal (it constituting a way in which certain things are looked at), yet it is factual and not merely verbal. To say that some social institutions or human relations are just is not just a way of talking about them (just as to say that a poem is a sonnet is not just a way of talking about it but also a way of pointing to its particular arrangement or structure). It is also a way of pointing to some of their characteristics which we may consider to be of value in human relations when we look at them in a distinctive way. Here therefore the suggestion is that we are not at liberty to define 'justice' just as we like if we are talking about a moral value and expecting others to accept it. We are free to do that, of course, if we make no other claim than that we are proposing to use the term in a certain way in our discussion, irrespective of whether it is acceptable to others or not.

Another reason for saying that the question of defining 'justice' is a verbal question may be that one feels that definitions of moral concepts one way or another make little difference to our practical moral behaviour. We may find that a rationally acceptable definition of justice shows the institutions of slavery to be unjust. But the actual moral problem is 'What shall I do to remove this injustice?' and there a definition of justice is unable to render any help. This perhaps leads some people to believe that a definition is a way of thinking about things, but has no practical significance since it does not say what we should do to deal with an existing problem. Our task therefore is to get on with the job in our hands, leaving the problem of definition to those who want to talk. But is it really so? Those who opposed slavery must have done so because they thought of justice differently from those who supported it. And what is a definition of 'justice' but thoughts—one's own and other people's—about certain states of affairs, thoughts that are gathered up and clearly formulated? I do not mean that the people who opposed slavery put their

[1] The distinction drawn here between form and content is entirely an aspectual one, not one between two separate entities. It is also a flexible distinction, for 'justice' itself may become the content of some other judgment.

C

ideas down on paper or told it to themselves or others in clear and precise terms. But in order to find slavery unjust or to start doing something about it, one must have some conception of justice, however unconscious of it one might be. This is where the philosopher comes in. He makes explicit what is implicit in the conduct of those who oppose an institution because they think that it is unjust, or campaign for a particular reform because they consider that the state of affairs sought for removes some of the existing moral evils. A philosophical definition is not a proposal for some eccentric use of a term; it is an attempt to formulate more clearly and precisely than is done in unreflective behaviour that use of a notion which satisfies (this at any rate is what the thinker who proposes a definition for the consideration of others believes) the value-attitudes of rational beings. To demand that a definition should not only guide our understanding of the nature of an institution when we wish to see if it is just or not, but must also tell us what concrete steps we should take if we wish to take action, is to refuse to carry the responsibilities of an intelligent agent. For this demand is virtually a demand that one should be able to go through life merely by following ready-made injunctions without ever having to think or act for oneself. He who demands this demands to be dictated and not merely to be guided. From the fact that a definition is concerned with facts it does not follow that all the wrongs of the world will right themselves once we have got hold of a satisfactory definition of 'justice'. A social problem is highly complex; it does not admit of a simple solution but needs a patient and laborious approach to its different aspects that are often concealed in a question that is simply put.

It might here be useful to see how a definition may guide us in dealing with a concrete social problem. Here we shall deal with a problem that concerns an aspect of the caste system. The traditional caste structure does not allow intermarriage between people who belong to different castes. There are still some people in India who oppose such intermarriage, not because they believe they are thereby serving the cause of injustice but because they think that justice can only be preserved by such opposition. Intermarriage is a blow to the whole caste structure. The question of marriage between people belonging to different castes is much more than a question of happiness of the people concerned, it involves a potential danger to the harmony and preservation of the society itself, for it unsettles existing arrangements. Justice requires that those who want their happiness at the cost of the stability of the society they live in are not to be encouraged. Thus runs the argument. Here 'stability', 'harmony' and 'preservation' are treated as concepts of intrinsic worth, and so they are. An unstable society characterized by internal discord and lack of cohesion would certainly not be a just society. Is justice then the same as preservation and harmony? The critic of inter-caste marriage who believes himself to be defending justice has to say 'yes'; for if justice is something different from these concepts, then one's defence of a system in terms of them is not necessarily a defence of justice. Let us assume that the critic is a religious man and in this assumption we shall not be far wrong. For, as a matter of fact, it is extremely unlikely that someone in India who believes in the justice of a traditional system like caste would not also believe in God. Now, let us ask the defender of this sense of justice a question. Suppose that a dictator comes to power and passes a law that no man is to worship God, for religious faith enslaves men's minds and makes them incapable of rational thinking and material progress. And suppose that he has the support of a powerful section of the population and the most important people in the police and military forces are also fairly under his control. Individual opposition would certainly result in self-destruction, and any attempt at organized opposition will divide the country into opposing groups and may ultimately result in civil war, causing serious unsettlement of the social structure. Must we yield to this law if we want to serve the cause of justice? The critic will hardly agree to this. He may, of course, say that this law is itself unjust, for it is directed at changing the society as hitherto existing. But then every law passed causes some change or other in the hitherto existing arrangements of society, and we cannot say that no law should ever be passed in any society. If the critic says this, his conception of justice is not just stability and harmony, it represents a state of absolute standstill. If it is said that a law should bring about only small changes, we have moved away from the notion of preservation *in toto*, and are simply saying that we should be discriminative when we want to change existing arrangements. Justice then means discriminative change so that there is no great disruption in society. Discrimination in terms of what? To say that only small changes are to be allowed sounds like a quantitative solution. But it is not. No quantitative difference between a big and small social change may be made in the same way in which we make a distinction between ten pounds of potatoes and two. A law can only be judged by reference to the kind of change it intends to bring about, not the amount of it. If so, justice is neither total preservation of existing structure nor quantitatively small changes of it, for we do not know what that means.

'Justice', of course, implies that no individual shall seek his own happiness at the cost of happiness of others. Those who desire inter-caste marriage cause unhappiness to people who want to preserve the tradition of caste. Equally, those who oppose this marriage cause unhappiness to those who desire it. Between the happiness of two people who want to live a common life without interfering in the daily run of life of other individuals (the issue becomes complicated if such interference is involved and needs a different approach) and that of those who are unhappy because rather big changes are happening to the traditionally existing structure of society, which shall we choose? If justice requires that every individual should have an equal opportunity for the fulfilment of his needs, provided that such needs do not interfere with the fulfilment of other people's legitimate needs, then we must choose the former. It may be said that the attitude of the critic has become so deeply ingrained in him that he cannot be happy when things go against it; the opposition he shows thus represents a need of his nature. Why is it not required by justice that his need should be fulfilled?

Here we shall have to make a distinction between needs and needs and in this the notion of 'legitimacy' guides us. Any urge or desire felt by any human being may be said to be a need. But when different needs oppose one another, we consider those needs to be more legitimate which we find to be most intimately connected with the fundamental tendencies—ordinarily known as instincts—of human nature. That these tendencies exist we cannot deny even though they may take many different shapes in adult life as modified by environmental influences. But it is not impossible for us to see their presence in human activities. But some psychologists tell us that human beings have some fundamental tendencies which are destructive and aggressive in nature. But such tendencies, even if natural, are not consistent with the conception of a society of individuals. It cannot therefore be considered legitimate that an individual living in a society should wish for the fulfilment of such tendencies. Those natural tendencies are therefore legitimate which are compatible with the conception of social life. And those amongst human needs which are intimately connected with legitimate tendencies are themselves legitimate which can be fulfilled in different individuals of a certain society consistently with one another under conditions of a particular nature. Justice requires that such fulfilment can legitimately be withheld from some and not from others only on comparative considerations of merit and demerit.

Now, if we compare the need of the critic with that of those who desire union with individuals of their choice, even if they belong to a different caste, we shall have no difficulty in choosing which is more legitimate. For the need of those whom the critic is opposing is intimately connected with certain legitimate natural tendencies, whereas the connection of the critic's need with any naturally felt tendency of a legitimate nature is not obvious. We may therefore say that this 'need' need not exist and if it did not exist the action of those whom he is opposing will not be inconsistent with the possibility of the happiness of others. The critic's need—not to experience opposition to his conception of justice which is not rationally defensible—is such that its very presence is inconsistent with the possibility of fulfilment of many human needs connected with legitimate natural tendencies. It is a part of the conception of justice that people can be treated differently in so far as their merits and capabilities differ. The theory that people who are born in a socially inferior caste are necessarily inferior in abilities is now exploded. Let us suppose that the acquired merits of these two people are sufficiently similar to ensure a happy union. It is still possible that, the social environment, which contributes to the shaping of attitudes and outlooks on life, being different for people of different castes, the marriage will be difficult to work out. But it is not then a question of justice. In any case, this has to be left to the individuals themselves and cannot be ruled by a general law. I have entered into this lengthy discussion of this question only to show that a definition of 'justice' (provided that we are interested in it as a concept of intrinsic worth) may help us to understand a concrete social problem from the moral point of view and guide our choice between two possible alternatives in a particular case—defending or opposing marriage between two people who belong to opposite castes.

I shall now consider another treatment of the question 'Are ethical questions questions of language?' as we find it in Wisdom's book *Other Minds*.[1] Wisdom considers that certain questions are not really questions although they look like them. They are not asked because of any doubt concerning matters of fact, for the answer does not and cannot make any difference to our beliefs regarding existing facts. 'Whether we say of someone who asks of a text-book case of a leprechaun-driven watch "Is there an invisible leprechaun here?" that he is asking a joking question or making a joke, is a matter of choice, though the peculiarities of what he is doing are better brought out by saying that he is not asking a question. To say this removes confusion as to what he is doing, prevents abortive efforts to meet his demands, in the same way that to say of someone who asks, "Can one keep a promise unintentionally?" that he is not asking a question, prevents abortive efforts to satisfy him.'[2] Again, the promise question dissolves into, 'Is it in a case exhibiting features $S \ldots S_{n-m}$ but not $S_{n-m} \ldots S_n$ proper to speak of promise-keeping,

---

[1] I do not say that Wisdom holds precisely the same view about moral questions in his other contributions as well.

[2] *Other Minds*, pp. 32–3.

where the usage of "promise-keeping" is not definite for such a case?'[1]

Here the suggestion is that whether we call this promise-keeping or not is a matter of deciding to use language in some way rather than another both allowed by usage (i.e. some would speak like this: 'If a promise is kept it certainly is a case of promise-keeping whether one intends to do so or not'; others will say, 'Although the promise is kept we cannot call it promise-keeping if the intention to do so is lacking'). But whichever way we may decide to talk, the action which is being viewed morally remains what it is and the answer does not make us any wiser about it. This seems to me to be obviously true. But I do not think that the leprechaun question and the promise-keeping question are of quite the same kind. If a watch behaves funnily and we say 'there is an invisible leprechaun in it' we are only expressing its behaviour in an imaginative language and are not expecting anything more concerning the watch than we already know of. If we say 'there is an invisible brownie in it' our purpose will be served just the same. Now, let us examine the promise-keeping instance that Wisdom has given us. A has promised to B that he will leave his property to him. But he leaves it to his next of kin, meaning his wife. Unknown to A his wife has died and as B happens to be A's next of kin, under the circumstances he comes into the property. Shall we say, 'A has kept his promise unintentionally'? This question is certainly a question of language in the way Wisdom suggests. But there may be a factual problem in this question—which is complex in spite of its apparent simplicity—apart from a verbal one. There are two distinct points involved in the keeping of a promise: (1) one's character as is revealed in one's taking or not taking steps so as to ensure that what has been promised comes to pass, (2) some definite state of affairs which may be expected to come into existence when one has made a promise. When A deliberately takes steps against the promised state of affairs, he cannot be said to have acted as is required by the promise he has made and therefore he is not the man he should have been. We can only say that the state of affairs which can normally be

---

[1] *Other Minds*, p. 32.

expected to come into existence as a result of his having made a promise has come into existence although A did not intend it to be so. All this is expressed in a summary way by saying that A has kept his promise unintentionally. If we think from this form of speech that we can think of A as a man, since the letter of his promise has come to pass, in the same way as we would if he acted in accordance with the requirements of the promise he has made, we shall be making a mistake, and a factual one, from the moral point of view. When we say that a man has kept a promise we do not merely talk about some results, we imply something of value about his character as well. In the case under consideration this implication is absent. It is possible that this question is asked because one feels a genuine perplexity whether everything is as it should be in this case although we are saying that A has kept his promise. It reveals that moral situations are complex, that our form of speech does not always adequately express all the relevant facts, and that further thinking may be necessary for someone to avoid confusing some facts with others. The question 'Can a promise be kept unintentionally?' is therefore not necessarily a fake one or one whose answer lies merely in deciding on a point of language. Wisdom, of course, does not believe that metaphysical questions—and I have an impression that he considers ethical questions to be metaphysical—are meaningless, only they are paradoxical. They cannot be answered by 'yes' or 'no' as is the case with factual questions, but need a different kind of approach. For metaphysical questions involve no factual problem, and arise out of some perplexity in using language in respect of facts that we are familiar with. As we answer such questions we do not learn anything new but gain a new awareness of a pattern of events.

It is not exactly clear how we gain a new awareness of a pattern of events without learning something new about it. If we are just reminded of things that we know but which are not consciously in our minds at the moment, the process should perhaps be referred to as 'remembering' and not 'gaining a new awareness'. However, if the character of a metaphysical question is what is expounded above in the quotation from Wisdom, I doubt very much if we should say that all ethical questions are meta-physical (some no doubt are). For in a metaphysical question familiarity with relevant facts in respect of which no doubt exists either on the part of one who questions or one who answers is presumed. For if such doubt exists, the question becomes at least partly factual. Can we say that in all ethical questions it is per-fectly understood by all concerned what are morally desirable and all that is necessary is to throw a new light on facts present through clearing up linguistic muddles? Our experience of moral questions hardly bears this out. But perhaps Wisdom would say that when we speak of something or other as being morally desirable, only that which we are speaking of from a moral point of view is a fact but its aspect of desirability is not. But then his interpretation of a metaphysical question becomes somewhat different. It can no longer be defined as a case of linguistic paradox, but something else. For a fact then becomes something which can either be perceived by our senses or verified under some controlled condition. Anything in human affairs which is not an instance of either of these two possibilities is not a fact. Judged by this standard, ethical questions are surely metaphysical but not necessarily paradoxical. If a question is such that its answer cannot be checked by sense perception or verified under some controlled conditions, it is not necessarily the case that it is asked because of some linguistic perplexity. Besides, Wisdom concludes about the metaphysical character of questions, so it seems to me, from their paradoxical nature, so as not to prejudge what amongst our experiences are facts and what not, but decide on the character of the question itself—factual or metaphysical—by examining if it makes any difference to facts or not. It will not be logical, according to this procedure, to say that ethical questions are metaphysical because the sort of things they deal with cannot be verified, as what cannot be verified is not a fact. For then we have already made up our minds as to what questions are meta-physical and are not deciding on the metaphysical character of questions by finding out if they make any difference to facts or not. On Wisdom's procedure one has to show that no ethical question asked involves any factual doubt before one can say that all such questions are metaphysical. This I do not think has been done. On the contrary, it appears that Wisdom himself at times believes that some ethical questions may sometimes lead us to knowledge of facts. Yet he still refers to them as metaphysical. 'Metaphysical questions are paradoxical questions with the peculiarity that they are concerned with the character of questions, of discussions, of reasons, of knowledge. But this peculiarity does not make it impossible to carry through the reflection they call for so as to reveal the character of that with which they are concerned and thus, indirectly, the character of that with which they are concerned is concerned—time and space, good and evil, things and persons.'[1] I take it that when Wisdom talks about the character of time and space, good and evil, things and persons being revealed, in this revelation is contained more than what all of us already know of so well that no scope for asking any genuine question about them exists. Metaphysical questions, then, may also be factual in some ways. If this is not what Wisdom means, he should have said that in answering metaphysical questions we are reminded of the knowledge that we have regarding matters of fact. Even so, it is still an admission that good and evil are matters of fact. If so, all ethical questions are not metaphysical, for it may happen that someone would be genuinely perplexed as to what is good under a certain circumstance. The upshot of all these is that all ethical questions do not have to be metaphysical, nor is it necessarily the case that every question asked is either metaphysical or factual. It may be metaphysical in some respects (in the sense of involving linguistic paradox) and factual in others.

In the light of what has been said so far, I would like to conclude that ethical questions are not necessarily questions of language.

[1] *Other Minds*, p. 259.

CHAPTER II

In What Sense is Ethics a Theoretical Study of Objective Facts?

The failure to draw a distinction between the particular moral code of a community, i.e. its social customs and conventions, and general moral principles of an abstract nature has caused a lot of needless confusion in ethical thinking. Social customs and conventions (like rules against belching, polygamy etc.), as their very names suggest, differ between different communities, depending on the special circumstances of their lives. Not so general moral principles like 'the truth ought to be told' or 'a life ought to be respected' which, I believe, have a general applicability to all human beings, even though we may have to limit their application to situations found more often in a certain community than in others. For they do not directly dictate to us any action in particular but stand for value ideals which human actions of many different kinds ought to realize. In this study the term 'Ethics' refers exclusively to general principles and not to customary rules. I wish to emphasize the distinction that holds between them, for what is true of general moral principles is not necessarily true of customary rules, although these latter are also known as moral principles.

Those who say that moral principles are not facts argue like this. Human beings behave as they do. The pronouncement of a principle that they should behave in this way or that gives us no more information about any behaviour with which we have concern than we already possess. If someone tells a lie, he does so; and we know no more about his doings by being told that 'one should not tell a lie'. This principle is therefore an expression of some feeling or attitude, or it is just an established behaviour norm of a society and not a statement of some fact which is somehow out there for all of us and which we may come to know if we probe into the matter. If by the term 'enquiry' we mean a process of investigation into facts which are there for us to know, then there can be no such thing as an enquiry into moral principles, for principles are neither facts themselves nor do they give us any knowledge concerning facts.

Now it is true to say that a principle is not a fact when by the term 'fact' we mean something that has a definite and particular nature identifiable as a distinct object, quality or event. But there is no reason why we must use the term 'fact' only in this sense. If we examine common usage we shall see that 'fact' is used not only in respect of observable and verifiable objects but also in respect of anything which demands acceptance and for the rejection of which there is no justifiable ground. Consider the following conversation: 'Is it a fact that you intend to undertake a world-tour next year?' 'Yes, it is'. If we accept this wider sense of the term fact and be not prejudiced in favour of sense perception we shall find it possible to say that a moral principle embodies a fact and that it gives us knowledge of facts.

That a principle may be considered a fact may be made clear by drawing on an example in Physics, for the word 'principle' is used not only in morals but also in Physics, and Physics is acknowledged to give us knowledge of facts.

Principles in Physics are discovered. But to discover a principle in Physics, like the Principle of Rectilinear Propagation of Light, is not, as Toulmin points out in his *Philosophy of Science, to find out new facts as ordinarily understood, but to adopt a new approach to facts with which we are already familiar.* When we say 'a physicist had discovered that light travels in straight lines' something quite different is meant from when we say 'Crusoe discovered that there was a man on the island' or when we talk about the Natural History discovery 'migrating swallows travel along great circles'. There is nothing in our ordinary experience which corresponds exactly to the physicist's notion of light; for by it he does not mean such things as lamps—the light of 'put out the light'; and illuminated areas—the light of 'the sunlight on the garden'. So also the word 'travel' here does not correspond to our ordinary notion of travel and the same idea may just as well be conveyed through the expression 'is propagated'. As Toulmin says, the introduction of the notion of 'light' as something travelling is not the simple literal discovery of something moving like the detection of frogs in flower-beds or boys in apple trees. The physicist's discovery is not a discovery to the effect that where previously nothing had been thought to be, in any ordinary sense, there turned out on clearer inspection to be something travelling —namely, light. Nor is it the discovery that light travels in one way rather than in another. 'Rather, the optical discovery is, in part at any rate, the discovery that one can speak at all profitably of something as travelling in these circumstances, and find a use for inferences and questions suggested by this way of talking about optical phenomena—the very idea that one should talk about anything as travelling in such circumstances being the real novelty.'[1] We have known the data for this discovery for a long time—these are our ordinary experiences of light and shadow, the practical skill and techniques which have been developed as a result of these experiences and the regularities of optical phenomena like the higher the sun rises in the sky the shorter are the shadows. 'The novelty of the conclusion comes, not from the data, but from the inference; by it we are led to look at familiar phenomena in a new way, not at new phenomena in a familiar way.'[2] The justification for this new way lies in this, that it is called for by the facts being investigated and its function is to provide explanations for certain of the things that happen. 'Until the discovery, changes in light and shade, as we ordinarily use the words (i.e. illuminated regions which move as the sun moves), remain things primitive, unexplained, to be accepted for what they are. After the discovery, we see them all as the effects of something, which we also speak of in a new sense as 'light', travelling from the sun or lamp to the illuminated objects. A crucial part of the step we are examining is, then, simply this: coming to think about shadows and light-patches in a new way,

[1] *The Philosophy of Science*, p. 20.   [2] Ibid., p. 20.

and in consequence coming to ask new questions about them, questions like 'Where from?', 'Where to?' and 'How fast?', which are intelligible only if one thinks of the phenomena in this new way.'[1]

The general statement 'light travels in straight lines' is then not—as we are apt to think all general statements are—a generalized observation report on physical regularities, like the statement in Natural History 'migrating swallows travel along great circles'. The regularities with which this statement is connected are already recognized, it only provides a form for the explanation of their nature. A principle is then a formal statement and not a statement (in the sense of being a report of such occurrence or state of affairs) about any particular occurrence or state of affairs with which we are directly in contact. To say that it is a formal statement is to mean that the sort of things it directly tells us about are ideals or possibilities we can conceive of, which we conceive of because they explain why certain of the things happen as they do in our experience. The notion of 'light-ray', for instance, is a theoretical ideal and not any actual beam of light that we encounter in ordinary experience. This does not mean, of course, that the notion of 'light-ray' is a pure figment of the imagination, as it is by its help that we begin to understand optical phenomena more fully than we did before, and its function is to explain why optical phenomena that we actually encounter are connected in the way they are. This notion, then, which is ideal in a certain sense is also factual in another as it provides us with a form or framework, as it were, within which to organize our understanding of optical phenomena on a higher level than what is contained in a statement which reports the occurrence of particular phenomena that we actually come across.

In a similar way a principle of morals does not give us any more facts, understood in a certain sense, about the actual conduct we are concerned with but embodies a characteristic way of looking at it which enables us to pass judgments of a certain sort concerning the conduct in question. A principle of morals is formulated in recognition of the fact that some people do actually act in some characteristic ways in situations of a certain sort and also

[1] *The Philosophy of Science*, p. 21.

of the fact that we do feel and think about such actions in a characteristic way. But the function of a principle is not so much to describe such thoughts, feelings and actions as to attempt to explain them in terms of some characteristic conception of value ideals to be attained through human conduct. In so far as this is the case, a moral principle or law may be said to tell us about a form or framework within which to approach human behaviour in a certain way rather than about human behaviour itself as a series of particular occurrences. Let us take, for instance, the principle 'one ought to keep one's promises'. The function of the conception 'keeping a promise' is to set up a value ideal of human behaviour which explains, in a certain sense of the term 'explain', the actions of those who fulfil a responsibility expressly undertaken by them in spite of the considerable discomfort and at times suffering caused to themselves as a result, and also the feeling and judgments of approval that we come across for such actions and disapproval for the contrary. One may try to realize this ideal through acting in many different ways as required by the specific situations in which actions take place and there is no sum of actions which exhausts it. One may visit a relative, return a book to a friend, pay some money to an acquaintance or do a thousand other things, all of which may be referred to as 'keeping a promise' by virtue of the fact that in all these cases the fulfilment of a responsibility expressly undertaken by an agent is involved. Yet when one is told to keep one's promises one is not asked to perform any of these actions in particular, nor all of them all together. The judgment 'you should have visited your sister-in-law yesterday as you said you would' and the statement 'you should keep your promises' belong to two different levels in our thinking about human conduct. One is a judgment which concerns the desirability of performing a particular act, the other concerns an ideal which many particular actions are required to realize when looked at from a characteristic point of view. But in so far as this approach puts an aspect on the actions concerned which it is possible for us to conceive of and accept as somehow called for by the actions concerned, the ideal statement embodied in the principle has a factual character as well.

No doubt it is quite possible for one to refuse to approach human conduct in this characteristic way and we cannot say that one must do so, meaning that one can in any way be compelled to do so. But this holds true also in Physics. No one is compelled to look at shadow-casting in the physicist's way. We may choose, if we like, not to ask any scientific questions about it. But there is a certain sense in which something would be lost if we did not accept the physicist's way of looking at optical phenomena, as our understanding of these phenomena would be so much the less for that reason. Similarly, if we refuse to approach human conduct in the characteristic way which is embodied in the moral principles our understanding of it will be so much the poorer. For we shall lack that insight into some aspects of actual human behaviour, and feelings and judgments that exist to the effect that it would be better if we acted in some way rather than in another even if that would not have led us to achieve some desired object. If A seeks to know something about X of B in the situation Y and B wilfully misrepresents the case a number of people will feel disapproval towards his conduct and judge that B has acted wrongly. Are these feelings and judgments to be accepted just for what they are or is it possible to explain why people think and feel like this? It is in the service of this explanation that the moral principle 'the truth ought to be told' is to be understood. The principle says, the truth ought to be told, as not to do so would be to violate the value which an individual's desire to know has for its own sake. It is then true, in a certain sense, to say that a moral principle gives us knowledge concerning human conduct, although, of course, within the context of the characteristic moral approach to experience and this approach has its backing in some of our actual thoughts, feelings and actions. This knowledge, however, is formal, for a principle does not state actual occurrences that we are in contact with, but provides us with an ideal conception which explains certain discernible features of what happens. Nevertheless, it does add to our understanding of human conduct; and an enquiry into its nature is, in a certain sense, an enquiry into facts that we are all capable of conceiving.

But one may still not be quite satisfied as to the objective character of a moral principle and a further question may arise. We recognize that in spite of the moral principle 'the truth ought to be told' it sometimes becomes necessary from the moral point of view itself not to tell the truth. Wherein lies the validity of the principle if it does not command obedience in all cases? I think that this objection arises out of an inadequate conception of the role of principles in moral reasoning and the nature of moral situations and it can be met by drawing on parallel instances in Physics. Let us take, for instance, a law in Physics, say Snell's Law—the ratio of the sines of the angle of incidence and refraction is constant. This law is not universally applicable to the behaviour of every substance to which it is relevant. But the substances which do not behave in the way the law suggests are not specifically mentioned in the body of the law itself. And the fact that the law is not applicable to certain substances is only taken to restrict its sphere of application, not to suggest that the law is untrue.

It must be obvious that even when we consider a moral principle to be a fact—which ought to be called a 'value fact' in order that it may be distinguished from non-value facts—we cannot mean just the same thing by calling both a value fact and a perceptual fact 'objective'. Yet there is a sense in which both of these may be called 'objective'. Perceptual facts are out there, open to inspection, and we come upon them or discover them by using our senses. We do not create a fact like a tree in bloom at the bottom of the road, but discover it. A value fact is not likewise waiting somewhere in space to be discovered. Do we create it then? We certainly do not create it in the sense in which we create a picture or a statue which comes to exist in space through activities of a personal nature. But the understanding of moral facts does involve a greater element of distinctively human participation than does the perception of an object like a tree, inasmuch as what we comprehend as right and good come to exist as such for us only when we take up a particular value point of view towards human activities, dispositions and states of affairs. (In other words the factuality of value facts becomes a fact as we approach them in a distinctive way.) This element of human

D

participation lies in the bringing into being of a dimension of value experience which cannot be approached through sense perception but can be emotionally felt and conceived as being of a certain character. All human beings, provided that they possess a certain degree of emotional sensibility and rational maturity, are capable of such experience (in varying degrees no doubt), as is shown by the fact that values of a moral nature are recognized by human beings everywhere in some form or fashion. At the same time it seems undeniable that there is an element of recognition in moral comprehension just as there is in sense perception. For the possibility of moral approach to experience is inherent in human nature itself and is not peculiar to any one individual or group, although some individuals or groups may be, at a certain stage, morally more mature than others. Not only that, just as sense perception is felt to be a necessary mode of human awareness if we are to know objects existing in space, moral comprehension[1] is felt to be necessitated by the existence of certain characteristic differences between human actions and dispositions (which, of course, exist only if we take up a certain value attitude towards them). This is why moral evaluation seems to be, for those at any rate who engage in it, a sort of natural (in the sense of not being foreign to one's nature) response on the part of human beings to certain things, and moral facts are felt (understood) to have a significance beyond the experience of an individual or group. These are the sorts of things which are meant by calling morality 'objective'. We somehow remain unconvinced when philosophers argue that morality is not objective, for the question remains at the back of our mind why should so many of us belonging to so many different ways of life make this particular type of approach to some of the facts experienced unless they are such as to call for it and our approach is such that it fits them. If it is true that there will be no moral facts unless

---

[1] It is more than obvious that moral values cannot be apprehended by our senses, but we can surely comprehend or understand what are the sorts of ideas they stand for, i.e. what function they actually perform in our value judgments of a certain type. And inasmuch as both sense perception and moral comprehension involve understanding of whatever may be the object or point at issue, it has sometimes been said that we apprehend (understand) moral facts.

human beings adopt a particular point of view towards a characteristic kind of issues that are being experienced, it is also true that human beings can explain the legitimacy of this point of view only if it fits in with or is somehow felt to' be called for by the nature of experience approached in this way.

But another difficulty still remains. One might wonder, 'How can the general statement of a moral principle really tell us anything about human conduct? A principle appears to have neither inductive nor deductive connection with it!' It is said that the functioning of a principle in moral life is not a logical process and there can be no philosophical discussions about it. A general statement like 'the truth ought to be told' is neither an inductive generalization from observed human behaviour, for some human beings sometimes do tell lies, nor does it enable us to proceed deductively to condemn every instance of human speech that involves a lie, for sometimes it is morally better that the truth should not be told. What can we mean by saying that a principle gives us knowledge of facts when there is no logical relation between them?

The point in this objection is this. The kind of knowledge a moral principle conveys about human conduct is not the kind of knowledge which a statement bearing inductive or deductive connection between facts gives us. If we have collected various instances to the effect that rabbits eat cheese and have never come across one instance to the contrary, it is logically permissible to say 'rabbits eat cheese'. This means that we are justified in considering it highly improbable that a rabbit would consistently refuse to eat cheese unless some special circumstances not to be found with rabbits in general are present to account for this refusal. Since there are various instances of human speech which are not cases of telling the truth the statement 'the truth ought to be told' is not of this nature. Again, we are so certain of the general statement 'men are mortal' (i.e. of the connection between humanity and mortality) that we need have no hesitation at all in inferring about a particular man that he is mortal. Since we do believe in some instances of human speech that the truth ought not to be told, the general statement 'the truth ought to be told' has not this deductive certainty either. How then can there be a logical passage between actual human behaviour and a moral principle?

Now it is true to say that the general statement of a moral principle is not an inductive generalization, nor does it reveal a deductive connection between observed facts. Yet it does not follow from these that a principle has no logical status in our thinking which enables us to draw conclusions of a certain kind which we may consider to be either valid or not concerning facts of experience. For this lack of inductive or deductive connection between relevant facts is a feature not of moral principles only but also of principles in Physics. The Principle of Rectilinear Propagation of Light in Physics, as Toulmin observes, is not a generalization from observed regularities. Nor does it enable us to infer deductively that light is travelling in straight lines from a particular source, for there are optical phenomena like refraction and diffraction which limit the operation of this law. What then is precisely the logical function of this principle in our thinking in Physics? Let us take a piece of reasoning in Geometrical Physics and see what is involved. Suppose that we know that the sun, from an angle of elevation of 30°, is shining directly on to a six-foot-high wall, we could infer that the shadow cast will be ten and a half feet deep on the level ground behind the wall. How do we infer that the shadow is just ten and a half feet deep: why not fifty feet or two?

' "Well, that's easy enough," the physicist will say. "Light travels in straight lines, so the depth of the shadow cast by a wall on which the sun is directly shining depends solely on the height of the wall and the angle of elevation of the sun. If the wall is six feet high and the angle of elevation of the sun is 30° the shadow must be ten and a half feet deep. In the case described, it just follows from the Principle of the Rectilinear Propagation of Light that the depth of the shadow must be what it is." '[1]

Now what sort of inference is this? Quite obviously it shows neither an inductive nor a deductive process of the traditional

---

[1] *The Philosophy of Science*, p. 24.

type and involves a novel method of drawing physical inferences, a method not recognized by books on Logic. This method is the diagram-drawing technique of Geometrical Optics. The physicist will draw a diagram in which the ground will be represented by a horizontal line, the wall by a vertical line and a third line will be added at 30° to the horizontal, touching the top of the line representing the wall and intersecting that representing the ground. The third line represents the bottom ray of light which can get past the wall without being cut off. All the lower ones are intercepted, which explains why the ground behind the wall is in shadow. The depth of the shadow in this diagram is one and three-quarter times the height of the wall, and if the wall is six feet high the shadow must be ten feet six deep. This diagrammatic technique of drawing inferences can be used only if we regard light as travelling. Of course, the physicist need not necessarily draw diagrams, he may resort to trigonometry or some other mathematical symbolism. But the characteristic way of looking at optical phenomena embodied in the principle 'light travels in straight lines' also brings with it characteristic methods of representation and techniques of drawing inferences. The principle itself, to use terms suggested by Ryle and Toulmin, is like a licence or ticket on the strength of which we pass from certain facts to others although this passage involves neither inductive nor deductive processes.

Now that we have the authority of science to the effect that a valid inference need not necessarily be either inductive or deductive it is perhaps easier to see how we can pass judgments of a certain kind on people's conduct and character on the strength of a principle or law which gives us a licence to reason in a certain way and consider such judgments to be tenable or not, in spite of the steps involved in this process of moral inference being neither inductive nor deductive. The moral approach to experience is a characteristic approach like the approach of Geometrical Optics—although unlike the latter it is as old as human thought—and it has its own way of drawing inferences.[1]

---

[1] I have developed this point further in a subsequent chapter where I have discussed the nature of moral reasoning somewhat in detail.

Nowell-Smith in *Ethics* objects to calling Ethics a theoretical study on two grounds. He thinks that moral knowledge can be represented as theoretical only if we admit a world of non-natural characteristics which terms like 'right' and 'good' are believed to stand for. Other philosophers have also opposed the idea that Ethics can be considered a theoretical study of value facts on the ground that the term 'value fact' presupposes a queer value world, a sort of world of ghostly entities, just as the term 'perceptual fact' presupposes a spatial world. But such a world is presupposed only if we insist that the term 'fact' has only one meaning—namely, verifiable through perception and a direct inference based on such perception. If anything is called a fact and is yet not verifiable in this way it must be because it has a ghostly existence to be perceived by the mind's eye (or in some such queer way). But there does not seem to be any reason at all why we must say that anything that is called a fact must have either a bodily or shadowy existence. It is enough—and this shall not contradict usage—if what is being called a fact is such that we find that it somehow demands acceptance and there is nothing which calls for its rejection. A fact like this exists only in the sense that it is possible for us to conceive of it and such a conception is somehow necessitated by the nature of our experience. The terms 'right' and 'good' stand for conceptions of value ideals of a characteristic nature to be achieved by human conduct and we are justified in calling them moral facts (unless we are going to confuse them with perceptual facts for the simple reason that the term 'fact' is being used) if these value ideals demand acceptance from us in the light of our experience. They do not need to inhabit a special kind of world, all that is necessary is that we should be able to understand the conceptions involved in these terms and find that we cannot get along with the valuation of human conduct from a characteristic point of view without their use, when such valuation comes naturally to us. To talk about the existence of value facts, I repeat, is not to talk about anything physical or shadowy, it is to talk about the function and use of certain conceptions which enable us to think of certain things in a certain way, when that is called for by aspects of our experience.

The other difficulty Nowell-Smith finds about calling ethical judgments theoretical statements is this. The truth of scientific statements—statements acknowledged to be theoretical—is either verified by an appeal to sense perception or there are tests by means of which we can decide whether a thing only looks or feels in a certain way or whether it really is what it looks or feels. What can be the test of truth in moral matters? How are we to choose between differing moral opinions?

Now it is quite true that ethical statements are not statements which may technically be called scientific, and that there are no ready-made tests by means of which we can forthwith resolve a moral dispute. But it is not true that there are not any standards at all involved in morals which our thinking is required to respect. Moral issues are so complex that it may not be possible for us to decide conclusively on the relevance for moral evaluation of certain facts present or isolate them from all complicating factors as we do in scientific matters. As a result our particular moral judgments about the same state of affairs (for instance, 'public ownership of all means of production is good' and 'public ownership etc. is bad') may oppose one another and the opposition may remain unresolved. Nevertheless whenever a particular judgment is claimed to be a moral judgment an attempt is made to show that it is in accordance—in circumstances of a particular nature—with certain general standards or principles which will be accepted as self-evident in the sense of not needing any extraneous justification for being acceptable as desirable states by themselves. For instance, those who demand public ownership argue (rightly or wrongly) that only this ensures social justice and they believe that the concept 'social justice' is such that it will show itself to all to be a desirable goal to aim at. Those who oppose the idea of public ownership argue (again, rightly or wrongly) that it interferes with the freedom of individuals to live their own lives, which they believe will recommend itself to all as 'not to be surrendered', stating at the same time that a gradual approximation to justice is possible without the adoption of such all-embracing means as are involved in 'public ownership' which is bound to create fresh injustices in its wake. Admittedly the arguments involved are far too complex for anyone to carry them to a conclusion which will have to be accepted by both sides. Nonetheless they show that appeal is being made to certain conceptions of self-justifying standards (or which are at least believed to be so) to justify the particular judgments passed. The theoretical study called Ethics deals not with the particular judgments but the conceptions of standards involved in these judgments, and their implications. And these standards, if they are to be accepted as standards at all, must be self-justifying and therefore would need no test of truth.

This no doubt will be profoundly disappointing to many who are interested in Ethics. For have we not saved the theoretical character of Ethics at the cost of reducing it to the reiteration of formal principles which may appear to be truisms to anyone who believes in the moral approach and which are not the objects of our actual ethical disagreements? No doubt; yet it seems to me that even to have done this is somewhat rewarding at the present stage of our ethical enquiry, for there are so many well-meaning thinkers who starting from the variety of irresolvable moral disputes end at suggesting that there are no such things as self-evident moral principles which we all must accept if we wish to respect the moral point of view.

CHAPTER III

Rationality of Morals

PART I   THE PLACE OF REASON IN ETHICS

It is often heard in certain philosophical circles that morality is not rational. Those who hold such a view only succeed in establishing that moral principles cannot be proved to be valid to anyone who chooses not to accept them by a process of reasoning or argument, i.e. by a process of thinking by means of which something which is not immediately accepted is shown to follow from or to be entailed in something else which is accepted as given in the context of argument. He who rejects moral principles rejects the whole moral approach to experience. One may be persuaded to make this approach, but more than arguments will be needed for it. One will have to be helped to develop a new insight, and to enlarge one's understanding of human nature and potentialities. But there is no reason why the term 'reason' will have to be taken as synonymous with 'reasoning'. 'Reason' in its widest sense includes insight into hitherto unsuspected relationships which reveal themselves to one's understanding (relationships which being fundamental cannot be deduced out of something else) as also a process that we may term 'reflection', i.e. a process by means of which we endeavour to understand more clearly and somewhat explicitly what is involved in the acceptance of an idea which is often unconsciously taken in and vaguely felt as 'not to be surrendered'. We reflect on an idea if it is not clear enough in the sense that its use in different instances leads to conflict or confusion or both but also only if we have already accepted it in some sense, whereas we employ a process of reasoning in order to establish something which is yet to be accepted. Morality may not be rational in the sense that fundamental moral principles cannot be proved to be so by a process of reasoning, yet it may be rational in the sense of 'admitting of reflection' or in the sense of being amenable to our understanding.

Toulmin believes that there is a place for reason in Ethics. But limiting as he does the conception of reason to reasoning or the advancing of grounds on which to accept a thing not otherwise acceptable, the place which he assigns to reason in Ethics is somewhat restricted and confused. He says in *The Place of Reason in Ethics* that there are two kinds of moral reasoning. (1) Reasoning which is concerned with justifying a particular action, and this is done by showing that it is an instance of an established practice or principle. (2) Reasoning which is concerned with the justification of a practice by reference to the ideal that suffering that is avoidable should not be tolerated. The sort of reason that is called for in the justification of a particular action is not the sort of reason that is called for in the justification of an established practice. That there is a distinction between reasoning about particular actions and reasoning about a practice is not to be doubted. But it does not appear to me to be as radical as Toulmin holds it to be. Toulmin is saying that once we have brought an action under an established practice we have given all the reason, and good reason at that, that can be given for its justification. Yet, an established practice is itself not beyond criticism. It can be criticized in terms of an ideal. If so, how can we accept that there is no more place for reason in arguing about the moral suitability of a particular action once we have brought it under an established practice? One would be inclined to conclude that Toulmin is suggesting that only a few, the moralists, should challenge a practice, while others should demand no more reason in favour of an action than that it is required by an established practice. And the fact that a practice is established is a good reason, except for a moralist, why an action which falls under it should be performed. This seems to me to be very unsatisfactory. How can a moralist challenge a practice while the rest of the people in the society follow it without question? The moralists, those who criticize an established practice with reference to an ideal, may be exceptional people; yet they must think, feel, and act in a social context. Their understanding of social affairs may be more comprehensive and their criticisms better-grounded and more satisfactorily formulated in so far as they are clear about the standards they are judging by. But they take shape in an atmosphere where there is already in evidence a considerable amount of questioning on the part of common people, however vague their understanding and ineffective and ill-expressed their objections. The reactions of a moralist do not mark the beginning of an entirely new understanding, rather they represent a culmination of a process of social awareness. Moreover, there is no specific criterion by which we can judge conclusively that an established practice causes a degree of individual suffering that is undesirable at a certain stage of progress (for living in society as we have hitherto had knowledge of, inevitably demands a certain amount of compromise on the part of the individual members) or that it is of a kind that is avoidable. Any social decision that is taken on these matters is usually preceded by many sporadic actions and objections on the part of different individuals. We cannot therefore make a hard-and-fast distinction between the questioning of a social practice by a moralist and the often vague and inadequate questioning by common people of particular actions even when they are known to be instances of an established practice. And what is important for us is to understand and reflect on the standards that are implicitly contained in such acts of questioning. Indeed, Toulmin himself suggests that there is no hard-and-fast distinction between a 'moralist' and an ordinary person and that we are all moralists in a limited way. If so, it is necessary for all of us to understand what the standards are by which the moral value of established practices is to be assessed and what is involved in the acceptance of such standards; it is not enough to know that certain practices are established.

Certain of the difficulties mentioned above could be avoided if Toulmin made a distinction between the conception of a social practice or institution which is relatively specific and particular in nature and that of a general moral principle like 'a promise

ought to be kept'. The case which he chooses to establish his
point that we cannot reason any more when we have brought an
action under an established practice is really a case of a principle.
If A says to B that he must take back a book to C on a certain
date, B might question why he must do so considering that it is
rather inconvenient for him. When A explains that he had
promised C that he would and a promise ought to be kept
there is no more scope for a further questioning of A's proposed
action for anyone who respects morality. We are satisfied that
this is the case, for a principle is a standard by which we judge the
moral value of particular actions performed, and this standard is
self-evident. What a moralist criticizes, however, is not a principle but a practice which is not so valid, and its moral justification can be assessed in terms of ideals or standards which we find
are acceptable for what they are, and this is to say that they do not
need any further justification. We cannot, so it seems to me,
satisfactorily understand the nature of moral judgments without
the recognition of the self-evident character of certain standards
that we apply in moral contexts.

   To judge a particular action to be valid because it is an instance
of a self-evident moral principle and to judge a social practice to
be undesirable because it tolerates avoidable suffering are not two
entirely different kinds of rational activities. For in both the cases
that which is given is judged in terms of an ideal, the only difference being that the principle 'a promise ought to be kept' embodies
a relatively specific ideal, while the ideal involved in the conception
'avoidable suffering should not be tolerated' is more general. But
both are ideals which can be further explained by the highly
general conception of moral 'ought' which is a conception in
terms of which all that is of value for human beings from a
characteristic point of view may be understood.

   It is because Toulmin pays little attention to the conception of
moral 'ought' that he seems to advocate that the question of
justification of a particular action cannot proceed beyond that of
an established principle. An individual in the English society
where monogamy is the established practice cannot, says Toulmin, sensibly ask 'Is it right for me to marry one wife or four?'

By implication an individual in a Muslim society cannot ask 'Is it right for me to have more than one wife?' For such a question is really a question about the whole way of life to which this practice belongs. A Muslim who is refusing to have more than one wife is questioning the institution of polygamy which really means that he is questioning the whole way of life of the Arabs and voicing his preference for an alternative way of life such as the Christian. This to me is not, however, quite clear. Suppose that an Arab tribesman is being persuaded to marry again when he already has a wife. Is there anything against his questioning whether it is right for him to do so even though his social system sanctions it? Again, is he necessarily questioning the propriety of the social system itself if he is questioning the propriety of several marriages in his particular case? Further, why must he necessarily question the whole way of life of the Arabs if he is questioning the institution of polygamy? The expression 'way of life' includes every aspect of social life and not merely the marriage customs. And in spite of different institutions of a society being interrelated a change of the whole way of life is not usually called for whenever a need for changing any particular institution is felt. Otherwise every reform would involve a radical transformation of the society in question. Says Toulmin, 'In general then if one is to reason about social practices, the only occasions on which one can discuss the question which of two practices is the better are those on which they are genuine alternatives: when it would be practicable to change from one to the other within one society. Given this, the question "Which is the better?" has the force of "If we changed from one to the other, would the change have happy or unhappy consequences on the whole?" But, if this condition is not satisfied, there is, morally speaking, no reasoning about the question, and pretended arguments about the merits of rival systems—personal preferences apart—are of value only as rhetoric.'[1]

It is not easy to see what Toulmin has in mind when he talks about change within one society. Society is not an entity that has a definite structure in any literal sense of the term. It is a conception in terms of which we explain the characteristic connection

[1] *Reason in Ethics*, p. 153.

that there is between different institutions, practices, laws, etc., of a group of people. To change any of these is to change the character of the society to some degree or other. Yet it need not involve a complete break with the society as hitherto existing, so that we may still refer to it as the same society. When we talk of one society we cannot mean anything which has an unalterably fixed structure, for few societies, if any, have this. We mean a body of institutions which although changing are changing in a manner so as not to lose completely, at any one stage of change, the connection that different institutions have with one another, and so as not to have the continuity that the present of an institution has with its past completely destroyed. There is no reason why the institution of monogamy cannot be introduced into a Muslim society without changing a Muslim society into a Christian one. And there seems to me to be good reasons why the institution of polygamy should give way to monogamy.

Given the conditions that women in a society far outnumber men and that the women concerned would rather share a husband with a few others than remain unmarried, polygamy has its social justification. But such conditions may not exist or they may change, in either of which case the practice of polygamy becomes morally objectionable. There is a conception of marriage according to which it is considered to be an exclusive relationship between two people based on recognition, consideration, and affection for each other freely and equally bestowed. Under polygamy the co-wives never realize the exclusive character of the relationship, nor do they ever attain the status of supreme personal importance shared equally with a partner in a joint life as a married woman under the system of monogamy has the possibility of attaining—while having no other alternative but to centre their attention on a man who is incapable, from the very nature of the case, of returning it alike. Judged by the standard of what is desirable and attainable in the relationship of marriage, monogamy is certainly to be preferred to polygamy. And unless there are specific circumstances in a particular Muslim society which not only make polygamy necessary but desirable under the circumstances, we are justified in saying that polygamy should not be practised now that the society practising it knows of a better type of marriage relationship, namely monogamy. We cannot therefore agree with Toulmin when he says 'The question "Which of these institutions is 'right'?" is therefore an unreal one, and there is no conceivable way of answering it—as it stands.'[1]

When Toulmin says that there is no more place for reason in Ethics after an established principle like 'a promise ought to be kept' has been cited in favour of a particular action, he appears to reject by implication the role of reflection in ethical understanding. A process of reflection is called for where one's understanding of an issue is not as clear as one wishes it to be, and this clarity is attempted by drawing out in greater detail what is implied in one's experiences in this connection as looked at from some characteristic point of view which one might confuse with some other point of view that is in some ways different from it (for instance, the point of view of moral 'ought' and that of convenience for the doer). It is our higher-level experiences (as against perceptual ones), those which involve complex distinctions to be grasped by the use of abstract conceptions, like efficiency and inefficiency, promise-keeping and promise-breaking, that are, when expressed in language, in danger of being confused with expressions of other related experiences of a somewhat similar nature. Reflection then is a process of thinking that is aimed at the logic of a highly abstract conception, used from a certain point of view, as distinct from the logic of arguments and inferences. What I mean is this. An abstract conception (i.e. a term which has no sensible counterpart) takes shape through our attempt to express some of our higher-level experiences, a level of experience at which we find ourselves whenever we are affected in some particular manner through the recognition of certain characteristic relations between features already experienced at a lower level. To understand how certain things are related in a characteristic way is to understand how they differ from everything else to which they are not being considered to be related. The logic of an abstract conception then consists in the recognition

[1] *Reason in Ethics*, p. 153.

of characteristic differences between certain features already experienced at a lower level (to be able to say, for instance, that
Miss A is an efficient typist one must have experiences of the sort
involved in the recognition of differences that there are between
the work of typists who make many mistakes, have relatively less
speed, etc., and those who do not make many mistakes, have
high speed, etc.). An abstract conception then can be defined by
explaining how the objects to which it applies differ in a characteristic way from objects to which it does not apply.[1] This shows
that a process of reflection is a process where reason is employed;
and if so, reflection on the logic of moral concepts (which embody
our experiences of moral distinctions) is a rational process. And
such reflection is called for in view of the fact that our understanding of moral concepts is by no means clear of all confusion.

We can now see why we need not say with Toulmin that there
is no more place for reason in Ethics once a particular action has
been shown to be the instance of an established principle like 'a
promise ought to be kept'. For there is still scope to reflect why the
conception of promise-keeping comes under the conception of
moral 'ought' or, in other words, what is the logic of this conception as viewed morally. There is, of course, no scope for reasoning,
for one either already accepts that a promise ought to be kept, in
which case argument is unnecessary, or one does not, in which
case it will be futile. For the conception of moral 'ought' is a
fundamental conception and it cannot be derived by a logical
process from something else of which the objector might have
an experience. If therefore someone says 'Why do you say that a
promise must be kept? One has every right to break a promise if
the keeping of it is very inconvenient. Can you prove that it is
wrong to break a promise?' we do not know how to answer. He
who is asking this question is refusing to adopt a moral point of
view, for when one adopts this point of view one no longer needs
a proof that a promise ought to be kept (this question is different
from the question whether a particular promise ought to be kept

---

[1] I should like to mention here that the recognition of higher-level differences is relative
to our purpose and that the logic of an abstract conception is flexible, depending on the
context in which it is used.

under a specific set of circumstances). We can only tell him why we consider that a promise should be kept, but this will appear satisfactory only if he has already adopted a moral point of view. A discussion of the question why we consider that a promise ought to be kept is not a useless discussion, for it shows that an established practice, institution or even a principle of some generality is not an ultimate fact in the sense that all we can do is to accept it. For a practice, principle or institution may more fully be understood in terms of the highly general and fundamental conception of moral 'ought' which expresses a level of experience at which we are affected in such a way by certain human actions, attitudes, and states of affairs that we feel an emotion of approval towards them which accompanies the thought that they are worthwhile for human beings for their own sakes.

Toulmin, of course, recognizes this level of experience when he talks about the function of ethical concepts or about what constitutes a good reason in the context of evaluating an existing practice. The function of ethical concepts, says Toulmin, is to harmonize people's needs and interests, which implies, although Toulmin avoids saying so, that a state of harmony is desirable for its own sake, which the existing state that is being judged is not. Again a good reason in favour of changing a practice is that avoidable suffering should not be tolerated, which implies that a state of affairs in human societies where there is no suffering is intrinsically preferable to a state which shows evidence of suffering. But these observations are not adequate to express all that is involved in the higher-level experiences that we call moral. The conception of harmony between people's needs and interests is no doubt involved in the use of ethical concepts, that is because the fulfilment of the needs and interests of a legitimate nature of individual human beings is morally possessed of value. When we recognize this we find that the conception of moral 'ought' includes more than the conception of harmony between people's needs and interests, it includes conceptions of certain attitudes and principles which are intrinsically preferable to their absence or opposite in human affairs. A particular action might then be judged morally, not in terms of how much harmony it produces,

E

which in any case may not be measurable, but in terms of the sort of attitude or principle of which it is an instance in a given case. Again, there are other good reasons why an established practice should be altered or modified than that the suffering it involves can be avoided. These reasons are connected with the moral requirement that the arrangement of social affairs should be as consistent as is possible under a specific set of circumstances with the conception that the individuals of a society should achieve as much happiness and sense of fulfilment as they are potentially capable of. Now it is not my intention to suggest that social affairs can be arranged in such a way that happiness would automatically be produced in the members of a society. For happiness, as we have conceived it here, can only be achieved by an individual, it cannot be given to him ready-made. Nevertheless, the arrangement of social affairs may more or less help or hinder individual attempts at achieving happiness, apart from more or less preventing avoidable suffering. And after all Toulmin himself recognizes this. For although he mentions only the negative conception of avoidance of suffering as a good reason in Ethics, he says that the moralist is also concerned with positively achieving a good life, which is involved in the conception of happiness as here adopted.

PART 2. IN WHAT SENSE DO WE INTUIT MORAL CHARACTERISTICS?

I have so far been suggesting that moral characteristics may become, in some sense, objects of our knowledge. How exactly is it that we know them? Quite obviously, we do not know them merely through using our senses, and some people would say that what we cannot know through our senses we do not know at all. As Strawson puts it in his paper 'Ethical Intuitionism' (presented in the form of a dialogue between North, an intuitionist, and West, an anti-intuitionist), they are a matter of what is felt in the heart, not of what is seen with the eyes or heard with the ears. 'Promise-keeping is right' resembles 'going abroad is exciting', neither of which is a matter of knowing anything. '. . . the only access to the moral world is through remorse and approval, and so on; just as the only access to the world of comedy is through laughter . . .'[1]

The argument appears to be that to say that we have some other access is to claim that we somehow know the facts that belong to this world. This is actually what is said by the intuitionists. Although I do not like to call myself an intuitionist, I hold that we do know some facts of moral nature intuitively when the term 'intuition' is understood in a certain way. I shall therefore first of all expound the sense in which I am using the term before I proceed to deal with the objections raised by Strawson.

Whatever meaning the term 'intuition' may have, intuitive knowledge has certainly to be distinguished from inferential knowledge. Inferential knowledge is mediate knowledge, i.e. in inference we accept certain facts on the authority of certain others. Intuitive knowledge is immediate knowledge, i.e. in intuition we accept facts, if we do so, for their being what they are and not because they are in some ways entailed in other facts that we already accept. Not only intuition but sense-perception as well can be contrasted with inferential knowledge, for in sense-perception too we accept facts for their being what they are and not because they are entailed in other facts. Both perceptual and intuitive knowledge then are, in a certain sense, immediate knowledge. It is, of course, understood that we use our senses in perception whilst we do not do so in intuition. Even so, the fact that both perceptual and intuitive knowledge are in a certain sense immediate makes us expect that intuitive knowledge would be rather like perceptual knowledge. That is to say, we expect that the object of intuitive knowledge would present itself as a simple quality of a non-natural kind before our mind's eye, as it were, in the same way as a quality presents itself to our visual or any other sense in sense-perception. We are disappointed when we find that we have no experience of any such mode of awareness and this naturally leads us to deny that intuitive knowledge is at all possible.

[1] *Philosophy*, January 1949, p. 23.

But there is no reason why we should expect intuitive know-ledge to be like perceptual knowledge in this way. The mere fact that we have two different terms 'intuition' and 'sense-per-ception' shows that there are two different processes involved. This does not mean, of course, that a process of intuition is something mysterious except in the sense that anything that is fundamental (cannot be entirely understood in the light of something else) is a mystery. I must make it clear here that I am not saying that any piece of human understanding is either perceptual, intuitive, or inferential. In our understanding of actual issues or things all the three modes of awareness are often not only present but indissolubly mixed up. In making the distinctions that I am making I am not suggesting that they are actually encountered in purity or isolation, so that if a piece of knowledge may be called perceptual it may not be called intuitive as well, and so on. The distinction is a distinction between recognizable aspects of our understanding of things rather than between the understanding of entirely different types of things. What then have we in mind when we talk of intuitive awareness?

Let us first see in a little detail some of the differences involved in our awareness of things. Suppose there is someone who knows nothing about electricity. He is shown an electric plug-point and told that he should not put his finger on it. He may agree not to do so but he does not see why he should not and the whole thing remains incomprehensible. But then somebody explains to him what electricity is and that he will get a shock if he comes into contact with it through the point. Now the man not only agrees but accepts in an understanding manner that he should not put his finger on the point. This he understands on the basis of another understanding about the functioning of what is called 'electricity'. It is therefore an inferential understanding, for unless one knows something about electricity one does not understand why one should not put one's finger on a certain thing which is an electric plug-point. But one cannot have this inferential understanding unless one also understands that a shock is not a thing to ask for. This latter understanding cannot be explained merely in terms of physiology, for although a shock is a nervous twitch, the understanding that this nervous twitch is to be avoided is itself not a nervous twitch. Neither can we call it an inferential understanding, for one does not accept that a shock is to be avoided because this is entailed in something else one understands better. Since animals as well as human beings avoid whatever produces shock it would be said that this is an evidence of instinctive understanding, and so it is. But it is important to ask what we mean when we talk about instinctive understanding. The term 'instinct' does not denote anything within us which can become an instrument of knowledge in the same way as our eyes or ears can. It is a term by means of which we explain the occurrence of certain types of behaviour which are related to one another in a characteristic manner and which are in some ways unlearnt. When it is said that we understand certain things through instinct what is meant is that we react towards the things concerned in our thoughts, feelings and actions in ways that may be considered appropriate to them from some point of view or other even though we have not exactly been taught to react in those ways, and even though we have not consciously figured out this appropriateness in our minds prior to our actual behaviour. Instinctive understanding is then in some ways an unlearnt recognition of certain features of our experience as being of a certain kind; and this recognition occurs not primarily through the instrumentality of the specialized function of any particular sense organ (although this may be involved) but through a total reaction of the organism to certain aspects of our experience.

What is called intuitive understanding is akin in some ways to instinctive understanding, although the issues that we understand intuitively are more complex than the issues that we understand instinctively. It is unfortunate that people are inclined to believe that to have an intuition is to be the favoured recipient of some esoteric knowledge in a mysterious way (thoroughly incomprehensible to people who are not specially favoured). I am of opinion that intuitive awareness is quite a common occurrence in human understanding, only the feeling that an intuition is not worth its name unless there is some mystery attached to it keeps us from recognizing this. I would say that any direct recognition of a difference between aspects of our experience which cannot arise *merely* through the function of a sense organ and yet which is acceptable as valid on its own evidence (i.e. it is acceptable for being what it is and not because of something else from which it may be deduced by a process of inference) is an instance of intuitive understanding. Let us take, for example, a difference of a complex kind which is grasped directly. To say that we grasp something directly may suggest that what we know forces itself on our attention in such a way that we cannot but know it to be there. This is because of the association of the word 'directly' with sense perception. If our senses are in order and we are not otherwise occupied, an object of perception forces itself on us so that we cannot but know it to be there. When I say that we know an object directly in intuition I do not mean we cannot but know it. 'Directly' here only means that we know the differences, when we do know them, neither merely as a result of perceiving anything nor of inferring it; it does not mean that we must know them whenever they are discernible in some sense. The word 'directly' or 'immediately' may also suggest that a process of intuition happens in a flash or that all of a sudden we become aware of things we did not know before. I am not using the words in this way, although it is not impossible for some knowledge to occur in a flash. There are certain complex differences to be found within our experience which we intuit (i.e. know directly) but a recognition of which dawns on us slowly and gradually. But however slow and gradual the process, in so far as it is a process of intuition it is not a process of inference. That we may intuit something slowly and gradually means that we, through a gradually widening field of experience and a slow seasoning of our personality to it, may ultimately get ready to notice certain discernible differences within our experience to which we were previously impervious. But when we do grasp the differences we grasp them as such and not as the derivatives of something else which we find are more directly acceptable.

Now, suppose that we know two people A and B, who are engaged on the same sort of job, say selling a particular brand of toothpaste. A is not easily put off, has a lively interest in the product, is always ready to take any pains necessary to convince others of the superiority of his brand and so on, while B, if not quite the contrary of A, shows little of the traits mentioned. We will then say that A is an industrious salesman while B is not. How do we know this to be the case? It is tempting to say that we infer this from their observed behaviour, but this will not do. For when we say, 'A is industrious', we are not imputing to him some quality which is additional to what we have observed about him; rather we are expressing the fact that we have grasped the unity or the characteristic relation that exists between the various ways in which A behaves in connection with his business, and that we understand this to be in contrast with the sort of behaviour that is exhibited by B. This I would say is an intuitive understanding, although it no doubt involves perception and inference in some ways as well. That is to say, the difference between industry and lack of industry is a characteristic kind of difference that we recognize directly and it is not revealed to us *merely* through our senses or through a process of inference, however much we may be helped to it through our perceptual and inferential abilities. In the same way, a moral difference, say, between considerate and inconsiderate behaviour is a character- istic kind of difference that we intuit or discern directly in some features present within our experience; and we discern this when we have noticed how certain types of behaviour differ from others in being respectful towards the individuals concerned as individuals and in recognizing the importance that whatever makes their happiness possible has to them. I have already remarked that to say that this characteristic difference between two contrasted types of behaviour is discerned directly is not to say any of the things; that it is revealed to each and all whenever the contrasted types of behaviour are present; that this difference presents itself in a flash and all of a sudden we come to know of a difference that we did not know before; that one is aware of exercising a faculty whenever one has an intuition other than the general human ability of discerning recognizable differences and so on.

But it may still be felt that I have not really explained the incidence of a moral intuition and it is still a mystery how it can happen. In a moral intuition, I have said, we recognize certain distinct characteristics of a type of behaviour in contrast to the behaviour of an opposite kind. What is the relation between these characteristics and the behaviour itself? Are these the properties of the behaviour concerned in the way sweetness is a property of sugar; and if so, why are we not aware of recognizing that an instance of behaviour, say X, is respectful to Y as an individual and mindful of the possibility of his happiness when we recognise that behaviour X is an instance of considerate behaviour? I do not know how far I am able to give a satisfactory answer to anyone who feels this particular perplexity. But the perplexity is surely occasioned by a category mistake. If by 'property' is meant a quality of an object like the sweetness of sugar that we perceive by our senses, then whatever is called a 'moral characteristic' is not a property, for by saying that we intuit it (in my sense of the word 'intuit') we have already said that we do not perceive it by our senses. What is called a 'characteristic' is something far more complex than a sensible quality, and is not out there in the same way as a sensible quality (which we are, theoretically speaking, in a position to receive whenever we are in the presence of the object and are not thoroughly absorbed in something else). It is what some philosophers have called a 'consequential quality'. This term may be interpreted in this way. An ordinary quality like the sweetness of sugar is something that we come to know directly through the instrumentality of our senses. We know it whenever we are in contact with it, provided, of course, we are not suffering from some physical or mental disability, and we have no difficulty in understanding other people when they refer to these qualities even when we are not in contact with them. This is because these qualities are there independently of any *specific approach that we may make to them*. These may, then, be referred to as first-order qualities for the sake of making a distinction between them and others. But there are other qualities, preferably to be called 'characteristics', which we may discern in the first-order facts (i.e. facts which are there independently of any specific approach to them) *when we take up a certain attitude*

towards them or when we look at them from some point of view or other.
These points of view (or attitudes) are value points of view—
whether instrumental or intrinsic. For instance, we may look at a
man working at a particular machine from a point of view from
which we wish to find out whether the man is discharging his
function efficiently or not, and this is because we prefer efficiency
to inefficiency or value it. If we decide to call the man 'efficient'
we are attributing to him a quality or characteristic which is
revealed to us not immediately, in the same way as sweetness of
sugar is, but when we approach the facts revealed relatively
immediately, in a certain way, take up a certain attitude towards
them, or look at them from a particular point of view; this then
is a higher-order quality or characteristic, it being noticed to be
what it is because of certain other things or qualities observed
more directly. A moral quality or characteristic is likewise a
higher-order quality which is discerned to be what it is because
of—or as a consequence of—our noticing certain other things
about a person's character or conduct, or about a state of affairs
towards which we take up a certain characteristic attitude.

This quality or characteristic is not then out there in the same
way as the sweetness of sugar is. But it is out there in the sense
that it is not a product of individual fancy. It is out there when
we have developed or matured in such a way that we are ready to
observe certain higher-order distinctions which are not apparent
at first sight. We can do so because we are—to press a traditional
philosophical point—possessed of an ability to reason and a
capacity to feel complex emotions. Let me now give an example
of what I mean. Suppose that shopkeeper Y charges price P
and shopkeeper Z price Q for the same article X (let us suppose
that the commodity is controlled and the price fixed). The
difference between price P and price Q is such that I could say
that shopkeeper Y has charged me more than shopkeeper Z.
Then I also find out that price Q is the controlled price for X.
Now when I have found the state of affairs to be of this kind, I
would also, supposing that I am ready or mature for it, recognize
another order of distinctions, the awareness of which comes in
the wake of awareness of distinctions that I have already found,

and it is this. The behaviour of shopkeeper Y as distinct from that of other shopkeepers I know is dishonest, and whether I am conscious of this to begin with or not, I shall find, if I reflect on this question, that I consider it dishonest in so far as it is characterized by being the extraction from me of more than I can legitimately expect to pay for the article involved. And I would not think that this sort of behaviour is respectful to customers. I would reflect in this way because I am somewhat indignant or disgusted at shopkeeper Y's behaviour. I come upon these characteristics through reflection and not through my senses, nevertheless these characteristics (of not being respectful to customers' rights, etc.) somehow qualify the behaviour in question; and these I implicitly recognize when I call it dishonest. If it would still be asked what sort of characteristic this is, I can say no more than it is what it is and that in the last analysis we know what it is not by abstract thought but by a reference to our actual experiences of moral distinctions. Again, if it be asked what sort of readiness is this readiness to find moral distinctions, my answer would have to be the same—it is the sort of readiness that it is and we can only understand what it is by reference to the ability of adult human beings, who may be considered to be normal, to make moral distinctions in contrast to the lack of such ability in people who are in some ways below normal or abnormal as also in children and animals. As to the relation between the characteristic and the behaviour in question, this is that the characteristic can be discerned whenever a behaviour like this is present, if, of course, we take up a certain value point of view towards the behaviour in question.

The next important question is: can we be mistaken in our intuitions? I believe that just as it is possible for us to have an illusory perception or to draw an unwarranted conclusion it is also possible for us to be mistaken in our intuitions. What then is the criterion for distinguishing a valid intuition from an invalid one? The answer again has to be disappointing. There is no formula by applying which one would automatically know a valid intuition from an invalid one, just as there is no rule by applying which one could automatically distinguish an illusory perception from a valid one. The question of criterion or rule is relevant only in mediate awareness, i.e. in inferential thinking where our contact with the object is indirect. In intuition, as in perception, we have to be content with accepting facts for what they appear to be unless there is a definite reason to think what the facts are not what they appear to be. An occasion for thinking that we may be mistaken is provided by our subsequently having a different perception or intuition of the same object or by our perception or intuition being contrary to the perception or intuition of other people. If our different perceptions and intuitions of the same object agree with one another and with those of other people, then to continue to doubt their authenticity is to misunderstand the nature of these processes as processes of human understanding. It might be said that even when no manifest cause to doubt the validity of an intuition exists, we cannot, in the absence of a test, be absolutely sure that there is no cause for doubt. Perhaps not. But as long as no cause for doubt is in evidence or can even be thought of on the basis of what we already know, we are justified in treating our intuitions as valid and this is all the justification we can have. It is sometimes thought that it is the feeling of certainty that attaches to an act of intuition which confers upon it the validity it has. But a feeling of certainty may be present in case of an invalid intuition no less than in the case of a valid one, although it is true to say that we are certain of whatever we intuit, when we have a valid intuition, even if we cannot offer a proof to the effect that it is valid.

No doubt it may appear mysterious that we have a feeling of certainty in respect of all our intuitions, and yet we are right in some cases and wrong in others, particularly when we have no criterion by which to distinguish the cases in which we are wrong from the cases in which we are right. But this use of the word 'mysterious' is different from the one in which we are justified in doubting that which appears mysterious, as in, 'it is mysterious indeed that you should be able to spend all these pounds on luxury goods when to say that you have no other source of income than your weekly £5 wage'. That we do have valid intuitions is not mysterious in quite the same way, for when someone says, 'I know it is wrong in general to break a promise, I cannot prove what I am saying, nevertheless I know by intuition that this is so', we do not think that there is any incongruity in what the man is saying although we may not think that we have any such intuition ourselves.

In the light of what has been said so far I shall now take note of the objections against ethical intuition as raised by Strawson. North, who is an intuitionist in Strawson's dialogue, expounds the intuitionist position thus: 'The fundamental cognitive situation in morals is that in which we intuit the rightness of a particular action or the goodness of a particular state of affairs. We see this moral characteristic as present in virtue of some other characteristics, themselves capable of being described in empirical terms, which the action or state of affairs possesses.'[1]

To this West, who is an anti-intuitionist, replies. A quality, say redness, is such that we can understand what it means by actually perceiving it in some object of our experience. It is therefore self-contradictory to say, 'I understand what the quality redness means but I do not remember ever having seen red, nor do I understand what it is to see red.' Similarly, if the word 'right' or the word 'good' expresses an indefinable intuitive concept, then it is self-contradictory to say: 'I know what the word 'right' or the word 'good' means, but not what intuiting rightness or goodness is like'. If intuitionism is true, then this statement is a contradiction. But it is not at all obvious that it is a contradiction.

To this I would say: the reason why Strawson does not remember ever intuiting rightness or goodness is that perhaps he means by intuition a non-natural encounter, and possibly a sudden one, with a non-natural property the recognition of which will be forced upon him and this did not happen to him. But neither has it happened to anyone who professes to have an intuition of rightness or goodness. To have an intuition of rightness is to come to recognize certain distinctions between contrasted types of human behaviour of a certain order, and this recognition involves an awareness which is in some ways non-sensible as

---

[1] *Philosophy*, 1949, p. 24.

well as non-inferential, and it is a recognition not through the instrumentality of any particular sense organ or part of our personality, but through our whole being, as it were. Anyone who talks about rightness and goodness meaningfully must have had a recognition of this nature. One may not remember the experience of having had a recognition of this nature, for it might have happened without one's having consciously taken any notice of it. But it surely is possible for one to know what it means to have a recognition of this kind.

To continue. The intuitionist North says, 'You intuit *that* an action is (or would be) right, a state of affairs good, *because* it has (or would have) certain other empirically ascertainable qualities. . . . The total content of your intuition includes the "because" clause . . .'[1] and it brings evidence in support of a verdict.

To this West replies, 'When the jury brings in a verdict of guilty on a charge of murder, they do so because the facts adduced in evidence are of the kind covered by the definition of "murder". . . . But the fundamental moral word or words, you say, cannot be defined; their concepts are unanalysable. So it cannot be in this way that the "because" clause of your ethical sentence functions as evidence. "X is a right action because it is a case of promise-keeping" does not work like "X is a salt because it is a compound of basic and acid radicals. . . ."'[2] Again, 'Generally, we may say that whenever q is evidence for p, *either* q is the sort of thing we mean by "p" ("p" being definable in terms of "q") *or* we can have knowledge of the state of affairs described by "p" independently of knowledge of the state of affairs described by "q". But neither of the conditions is satisfied by the q, the "because" clause of your sentence.'[3] The because clause then does not constitute evidence for an ethical judgment. West then goes on to say that as ethical judgments are not infallible we must have some evidence in their favour, if we are to say that these judgments are of the nature of knowledge. 'For to call such a judgment "non-infallible" would be meaningless unless there were some way of checking it; or confirming or confuting it, by producing evidence for or against it.'[4]

[1] *Philosophy* 1949, p. 26.   [2] Ibid., p. 26.   [3] Ibid., p. 27.   [4] Ibid., p. 27.

Now to take up the remark of the intuitionist first. We intuit an action to be right or wrong because it has certain empirically ascertainable qualities which act as evidence in its favour. For instance, we intuit that shopkeeper Y's action is dishonest and, which is the same thing, morally wrong, because it is an instance of deceptively over-changing. Does this 'because' clause which is empirically ascertainable or does it not provide evidence for the moral intuition and the judgment that the action is wrong? It seems to me quite evident that it does, if we understand the word 'evidence' in a moral context. The 'because' clause in a moral judgment, says West, does not function in the same way as in a legal judgment, where the jury brings in a verdict of guilty because the facts adduced in evidence are of the kind covered by the definition of murder. But the fact that a 'because' clause in a moral judgment functions differently from a 'because' clause in a legal judgment does nothing to show that the 'because' clause in a moral judgment could not provide the sort of evidence that is required in a moral context. Admittedly 'X is a right act because it is a case of promise-keeping' does not work like 'X is a salt because it is a compound of basic and acid radicals'. But what does this prove? It is a recognized fact that moral contentions, however tenable, cannot be proved to anyone who refuses to accept the point of view of morality. And it is only a person who refuses to accept the point of view of morality who would not consider that the statement 'X is an instance of promise-keeping' is a good enough evidence, in principle, in favour of the judgment 'X is a right act'. Let us suppose that X represents an action of leaving a certain sum of money to a relative who was given to understand that the money would be left for him. When we say that this action is right because it is an instance of promise-keeping we are not offering whatever is called promise-keeping as evidence in favour of the rightness of the act of leaving the money in any ordinary sense (as freezing of water would be evidence for the fall of temperature). Rather we are saying that this act of leaving the money is an act of promise-keeping because (i.e. we are here explaining what it means to say that it is an act of promise-keeping) it involves the fulfilment of an expectation intentionally aroused in another. And in so far as it involves this, this act is a type of act which we value from the moral point of view, which is the same thing as calling it right, because (here we are explicating what is involved in our valuing it) it is by fulfilling such an expectation as against frustrating it that we respect a person with whom we have dealings, and recognize a need of his which appears nothing but legitimate. Thus, in one of the senses mentioned by Strawson in which q may be an evidence for p, namely the sense in which q is the sort of thing that we mean by p, promise-keeping (q) is evidence for the rightness of the act of leaving a certain sum of money to the relative (p). For the paying of respect by one person to another in some definite way, or the recognition of a certain sort of legitimate need of a person with whom one has dealings in some special way, which is what promise-keeping is as viewed morally, is the sort of thing that we mean by the rightness of the act of leaving the money.

No particular ethical judgment is, of course, infallible. For although the relative was told about the money, is it possible that under certain extraordinary circumstances it would be morally better not to leave the money to him. The judgment 'the man's act of leaving the money to his relative is right as he promised he would' then may become an untenable judgment or at least a less tenable one than another judgment. But if the sort of things we have talked about in the above paragraph constitute evidence (moral) for an ethical judgment, then the untenability (or comparatively less tenability) of a moral judgment is not decided upon entirely without any evidence whatsoever. We can say that the man's act of leaving the money even when it is the fulfilment of a promise is morally wrong only when we have reason to think that by paying respect to the promisee through the fulfilment of the particular promise made, the man has committed a disproportionately great act of disrespect towards somebody or other, also involved in the act (it might even be the promisee himself in another capacity), and has overlooked the legitimate needs and interests of far greater urgency and importance that have a claim on him, also to be found in the situation.

To continue with anti-intuitionist objections. 'Of course these judgments are corrigible; but not in the way in which the diagnosis of a doctor is corrigible; rather in the way in which the musical taste of a child is corrigible. Correcting them is not a matter of *producing evidence for them* or their contraries, though it is (partly) a matter of giving reasons for them or their contraries.'[1] 'Of course, as you said, when we produce our reasons we are not often simply giving the causes of our emotional condition. But neither are we producing evidence for a verdict, for a moral diagnosis. We are using the facts to back our attitudes, to appeal to the capacity of others to feel as we feel, to respond as we respond.'[2]

Now the corrigibility of a doctor's diagnosis and that of the musical taste of a child are, quite obviously, different in some ways; for the doctor's diagnosis is a non-value affair whereas the musical taste of a child is a matter of developing a sense of value. But they are not entirely dissimilar in every possible way. A doctor's diagnosis may be shown to be wrong by reference to certain facts not hitherto taken notice of, a boy's musical taste may be improved by helping him to learn to appeal to more satisfactory standards of evaluation than he has hitherto been used to; and a standard of evaluation may be referred to as a value-fact in the sense that it is this standard as against anything that opposes it that is acceptable in a certain context of evaluation. We can, says Strawson, give reasons why a certain kind of taste in music is a better taste, but if the reasons be such that the kind of taste that is being recommended is accepted as a better sort of taste then this is all the evidence that is needed or can be given in such matters which belong to a value context. In any case, when we offer reasons of this kind we certainly do more than use the facts 'to back our attitudes, to appeal to the capacity of others to feel as we feel, to respond as we respond'. We also say that the attitude we are recommending is the sort of attitude that fits the facts concerned best from a certain value point of view. This is not only true about musical taste but also about moral distinctions. So there can be such a thing as a moral

---

[1] *Philosophy* 1949, pp. 27–8.   [2] Ibid., p. 28.

diagnosis after all, though we shall be disappointed if we tried to understand it in the model of medical diagnosis.

Now if moral intuitions are fallible we cannot assert as a necessary synthetic proposition, 'All acts of promise-keeping are right'. But if we intuit the moral characteristic rightness in an instance of promise-keeping there must be some sort of a necessary connection between rightness and promise-keeping. We can, says North, who is an intuitionist, assert as a necessary synthetic proposition, 'all acts of promise-keeping tend as such to be right'. And we derive our knowledge of such general necessary connection from seeing or intuiting in particular cases that the rightness of an action or the goodness of a state follows from its being an action or state of a certain kind. To this West replies: all As tend to be Bs, simply means most As are Bs. If the moral characteristics follow from some empirically ascertainable features of the action or state then they must always do so. If the characteristics follow in certain cases and not in others then the connection is not necessary.

To this remark of West I would say: there is a way of interpreting 'all acts of promise-keeping tend as such to be right or to have prima facie rightness' which does not result in the dissolution of the necessary connection that an intuitionist talks about between rightness and promise-keeping. Promises are made in actual circumstances of life which may be of many different kinds, and which may show relevance of a moral nature in many different ways. The rightness of promise-keeping belongs to that particular feature of an actual situation which is the intentional raising of an expectation in another and the undertaking of fulfilling it. In so far as this feature is present in any actual situation the action of fulfilling what has been undertaken fits it from the moral point of view. And this fittingness of this action to this feature of a situation is of a necessary character, i.e. we cannot say that sometimes the action of fulfilling what has been undertaken, and sometimes the action of not doing so, fits from the point of view of morality that particular feature of a situation which can be expressed by saying, 'someone has aroused in another an expectation and has undertaken to fulfil it'. What

F

actually happens is that some particular circumstance which presents this feature also presents another feature of moral relevance which cannot be respected if this feature is to be respected and then the action of promise-keeping does not fit this situation considered in the totality of its moral aspects, if the other feature appears in some ways to have a greater claim on the moral agent. 'All acts of promise-keeping tend as such to be right' then is a statement about the actual acts of promise-keeping as performed in concrete situations of life and not about the activity itself called promise-keeping which considered in abstraction from concrete and particular situations of life appears to be the only act that fits a possible feature present in a situation —and is in that respect possessed of rightness—namely, that a promise has been made. West, of course, might reply to this that the characteristic which we intuit as morally good or right is then no longer a characteristic which we find to be what it is because of certain empirically ascertainable features of a situation. For the rightness of promise-keeping has now become an abstract conception of rightness that has nothing to do with actual situations of promise-making and promise-keeping, and in so far as this is the case it is no longer a characteristic that can be found in the empirically ascertainable features of a situation. So the judgment 'promise-keeping is right' no longer expresses a synthetic necessity concerning our experience.

The force of this objection lies in the vagueness of the expression 'empirically ascertainable'. It is true that our conception of the rightness of promise-keeping as such is not derived from an examination of all the features that are present in any actual situation in which a promise may be kept. But the feature of a situation because of which the characteristic rightness belongs to the act of promise-keeping is an empirically ascertainable feature in the sense that it is found to belong to situations which are within our actual experience; and it is that someone has intentionally raised an expectation in another and has undertaken to fulfil it. But although this feature is empirically ascertainable, perhaps it is not empirically ascertained on any actual occasion of intuition of the rightness of promise-keeping. What I mean is this. When we have an actual intuition of the rightness of promise-keeping, it is not because we have consciously sought out the features of a situation and have found one because of which the characteristic rightness belongs to promise-keeping; but rather because we have been confronted with an actual situation, the most predominant or the only moral feature of which is the feature we are talking about, and it has struck us that an act which is an act of keeping a promise is the act that fits it morally, which is another way of saying that it has struck us that the moral characteristic rightness belongs to an act which is an act of promise-keeping. We are struck in this way when we adopt a certain point of view (that of morality) towards the feature in question, which means that the moral characteristic is not just given or found in experience in the same way as sensible properties are given or found in experience. It is given or found in experience when we are ready to take up a certain point of view—and this readiness presupposes a greater degree of maturity than is involved in our ability to receive sensible impressions—which means that we are in a position to adopt a certain point of view towards our experience and are not mere recipients. Why we must adopt this point of view is a question that I cannot answer, and whatever mystery there is in our doing so remains insoluble as far as I can see. All I know is that adult human beings who are not markedly abnormal or below normal do adopt this point of view, at times and in certain respects, at any rate. When we have adopted this point of view, a moral feature of a situation becomes an empirically ascertainable feature (in the sense that we can find it in our experience) and the fittingness that a certain kind of action is found to have to it expresses a synthetic necessity. That is to say, when we adopt a certain point of view the fittingness that a certain kind of act is found to have to a certain sort of feature of a situation appears to be a fittingness that holds in respect of other possible situations in which the feature in question is the most predominant moral feature. But the necessity remains a purely analytical necessity, i.e. a matter of how you define rightness, so long as the point of view of morality is not adopted. The rightness of promise-keeping is, no doubt, an abstract conception in so far as we cannot deduce from it our conclusions regarding whether or not promises as they appear in actual circumstances of life ought to be kept, but it still pertains to experience in so far as the feature because of which this characteristic is found is a feature discernible in some actual situations of life.

The intuitionist, North, says that we derive our knowledge of general necessary connection between rightness and acts of promise-keeping by seeing that the rightness of a particular act follows from its being of a certain kind. I would say that the word 'derive' here might be misleading, for it may lead us to think that we see or intuit a particular necessary connection first and then subsequently arrive at a general necessary connection. But a connection can appear to be a necessary connection only when we implicitly recognize the generality that is involved in it. That is to say, we can find that a particular act which is an act of keeping a promise is the only act that is fitting to this feature of a situation, namely, one has intentionally aroused an expectation, etc., only by recognizing implicitly that this act is fitting to this feature whenever this feature is to be found. It is only the explicit recognition of the generality of this connection that comes later. A moral intuition is then fundamentally a recognition of a general necessity of a certain sort which is involved in the presence of the sort of characteristic that is called moral.

CHAPTER IV

The Decision, Attitude and Command Theories of Morals

I shall now examine several theories of morals which, by suggesting that what moral judgments are concerned with are decisions, attitudes, commands and so on, imply that they are not concerned with facts. My criticism affects these theories only in so far as they may be taken to imply this. I have no wish to suggest that these theories have not, in their own ways, made valuable contributions to a better understanding of morals.

PART I. THE DECISION THEORY OF MORALS

Some philosophers believe that it is through the concept of 'decision' that we understand the nature of morals. Decision no doubt is a fact of very first importance in our practical moral experience. But philosophically the question is: can we explain the characteristic nature of morality by reference to the fact that certain situations in our lives demand that we should make a choice between possible alternatives? Or is it that the morality of any decision has itself to be understood by reference to something that is of intrinsic moral value? If so, we cannot explain the fundamentals of morals merely by stressing the importance of decision in moral life, even though the element of decision in moral choice needs all the stress that we can give it from the point of view of moral practice.

A theory which denies that moral principles (or what are called normative laws) can in any way be considered to be facts is apt to make decision the central point in morality. The function of normative laws is to guide our choice between alternative courses of actions which result in our taking a decision. Natural laws deal with facts and are statements describing regularities of nature. These two kinds of laws, says Prof. Popper, have hardly more in common than a name. A distinction has therefore to be made between (*a*) natural laws, or laws of nature, or positive laws, such as the laws of the apparent motion of the sun, or the law of gravity; and (*b*) normative laws, or standards, or norms, i.e. rules that forbid or demand certain modes of conduct, or certain procedures. Popper wishes to reserve the name 'natural' for laws of type (*a*) and says that we can speak of 'natural rights' or of 'natural norms' when laws of type (*b*) are meant.

Now it is not to be denied that there is a distinction of fundamental character between normative laws or principles and statements describing regularities of nature as dealt with in empirical sciences, for the former relate to a value point of view and the latter do not. But it is not true that those who have considered normative laws to be natural in some sense or other have confused them, as Popper suggests, with statements which we find in empirical sciences. In fact, the terms 'nature' and 'natural' are ambiguous. Clarke believed that what are morally right or good belong to the very nature of things and thus represent facts to be known by intuition. But then his conception of nature is very different from that of a physicist. 'Nature of things' stands for the whole of God's creation and this includes human beings with a sense of values. A moral principle is natural according to this conception of 'nature of things' not because it stands for any observed regularity in the non-human world (i.e. 'natural' in one of its senses) but because it is acceptable, and its contradictory is not, from the very nature of the case, to a rational being looking at conduct from a value point of view. Popper, however, thinks of nature exclusively in the sense of physical regularities. But the fact that Popper is using the term 'natural' differently from Clarke does not show that those who talk about norms being in some sense or other natural are mistaken. It is well to remember here, of course, that Clarke and observations similar to his are concerned not with conventional moral views whose rightness, if they are right, often can only be understood by reference to the tradition and way of life of a particular community, but with general principles which can be found to be self-justifying to any rational being with a sense of value.

How difficult it is to get rid of the notion of naturalness in morals can be seen from Popper's own statements. The confusion between natural laws and normative laws is quite unnecessary, says Popper, since it is easy to speak of 'natural rights' or of 'natural norms' when laws of type (*b*) (i.e. normative laws) are meant. If these laws have nothing in common with natural laws rightly so called except the name law, one would like to ask what would be the criterion of discerning what amongst our rights, obligations and principles are natural; and it does not seem to me that a decision theory gives us any such criterion. Indeed, it is difficult to see what Popper can mean by natural rights or norms. His theory of 'duality of facts and norms' sets forth that norms are by nature different from things that may be called natural. Why should we wish to say that laws that are by definition not natural have a natural character?

One would, of course, not wish to hold that general moral principles can be derived from any observed regularity of facts, natural or otherwise. For as Moore showed long ago in his refutation of naturalism 'what ought to be' is something different from 'what is'; and this difference lies in the fact that 'what ought to be' supposedly stands for something which we may consider to be of value when approached rationally, whereas what simply is makes no such claim. But it does not follow from the above that what is valued cannot be considered to be a fact, although, as is obvious, of a qualified kind. Why then can we not say that normative laws express the nature of value facts?

A theory of absolute dualism between facts and norms—one may recognize the distinction that there is between a statement of observed regularity and a statement concerning what ought to be and still not believe in absolute dualism—is fraught with grave dangers as it lacks any criteria provided by the nature of things by which moral decisions can themselves be valued. And nobody would deny that a valuation of our decisions is possible and indeed sometimes necessary. '. . . we can,' says Popper, 'compare the existing normative laws (or social institutions) with some standard norms which we have decided are worthy to be realized. But even these standards are of our own making in the sense that our decision in favour of them is our own decision, that we alone carry the responsibility for adopting them.'[1] Here Popper is making a distinction, notwithstanding his theory of critical conventionalism, without the recognition of which no theory of morals can do justice to the whole field of our moral experience—between conventional moral rules or practices connected with established institutions of a particular society and moral standards which are more than conventions. Conventional moral practices (to say that they are conventional is not necessarily to say that they are not moral) no doubt take shape through the decisions of generations belonging to a particular society. But they are moral not because of the decisions involved but because, as Popper says, of their being in accordance with certain standard norms. But what about these standard norms themselves? Popper says that the standard norms are those which we have decided are worthy of being realized. But these norms do not become standards of our judgments by reference to which conventional practices are to be judged through our decision. On the contrary we decide in favour of them as ultimate courts of appeal in our moral judgments by recognizing that they represent facts which are in some sense natural (i.e. not conventional). The standards, says Popper, are not to be found in nature. True enough if by 'nature' is meant the physical universe, but they are found in 'nature' if the term includes *the sense of values* of beings who are capable of reasoning and reflection. It is one thing to remember the important distinction between non-value facts and value facts and another to advocate that all norms including those of the highest generality, which Popper refers to as standard norms, are conventional or artificial.

Critical conventionalism, Popper is careful to stress, does not assert that norms are, at any historical period, consciously introduced by men, or that they are not of importance. It has nothing

---

[1] *The Open Society*, vol. i, p. 52.

to do with the assertion that norms are merely arbitrary. Yet it must be admitted, says Popper, that there is an element of arbitrariness in norms; but he does not make it quite clear exactly in what sense he is using the term 'arbitrary' which is ambiguous. All he says is that there may not be much to choose between two existing codes. This use of the term is very different from the one according to which a decision would be arbitrary if it does not pay respect to all the facts relevant to the situation. There is no element of arbitrariness to be necessarily recognized in morals according to this latter use of the term. By using the term 'arbitrary' Popper probably means 'made by men's fiat and therefore decided'. Now even if we accept it that Popper is talking only of conventional moral rules and not of principles, it is rather difficult to justify the use of the word 'arbitrary' in this sense if we are going to say that all moral rules are arbitrary. For some moral rules grow rather than being the product of a conscious decision and command of anyone in particular. It may, of course, be said that such moral rules represent decisions of generations but then the word 'decision' has somewhat changed its meaning. For what Popper is advocating is a conscious decision on the part of an individual agent to act according to a norm or not to do so. The norm itself is not a product of decision in the same way and is therefore not arbitrary in the sense that it is 'to be decided by one's liking', 'dependent on will or pleasure', 'at the discretion of anyone', 'derived from mere opinion or preference' and so on (see the Oxford Dictionary). The term 'arbitrary' suggests caprice; if a norm takes shape through decisions of generations, it cannot be said to be determined or regulated purely by caprice, for the mere fact that generations have agreed in deciding to accept a certain norm as a standard suggests that it is possible that the norm has satisfied a certain moral demand in some way or other in circumstances of a specific character for at least a number of people in the community at some particular time. As circumstances, aspects of the character of the society, and the moral awareness of people change, it becomes necessary to change the norm into something which is more satisfying to the moral demands that are present under the changed conditions; although it often happens that due to the abhorrence with which a great many people regard any unsettlement or change such a norm lingers on for generations. This only shows that a certain norm may become arbitrary at a certain time, but not necessarily that a particular norm that ought to be changed now has always been arbitrary.

The Oxford Dictionary defines 'arbitrary' also as 'not based on the nature of things'. But we have already seen that it depends on what meaning we give to the expression the 'nature of things'. I would say that norms, some at any rate, are based on the nature of things if 'nature of things' includes human nature that pays respect to the conception of intrinsic value. But I shall discuss this question later. The other meaning of 'arbitrary' as given by the Oxford Dictionary is 'not fixed' or 'varying', and norms, some at any rate, are arbitrary in this sense. Even so, they are not varying according to one's own liking or preference. In order to be deemed morally satisfactory they have to vary in accordance with certain conceptions of value.

There is a possible sense, of course, according to which all moral codes as actually existing may be said to be arbitrary, for no society has achieved the ideal which embodies the highest conceivable value in human conduct. But it is not the sense in which Popper uses it. In any case, the highest moral ideal—that of organizations of life in which opportunities for the happiness of an individual in conformity with the happiness of all others are fully provided for—is so very general that different kinds of institutional practices may be compatible with it depending on the circumstances and the people concerned. Again the same practice may assume different values under two different circumstances. Thus, of two different codes or practices neither may be arbitrary and the same code may be arbitrary in some situations and not in others. But here the arbitrariness or otherwise of a practice is judged in accordance with some criterion and is not considered to be an ultimate fact. Leaving aside the sense in which all moral codes are arbitrary, we judge established practices or codes to be arbitrary when we not only know that they fall short of the conceivable ideal but also can think of alternatives humanly attainable at the moment of decision which, we have reason to think, realize the ideal better than the prevalent practices do. In this sense moral codes and practices are more or less arbitrary and not all equally arbitrary; and a realizable practice which appears to be the least arbitrary at a certain stage also appears to be the best.

But this arbitrariness is a feature of what can be called 'the morality of custom and convention' which includes institutional practices but not of general moral standards which stand for self-justifying moral values. Critical conventionalism fails to make this all-important distinction between our moral standards, those that are conventional and those that are not and are in that sense natural. Although Popper does not clearly distinguish between moral rules (which are related to the conventions of particular societies) and principles (which are rationally defensible by human beings everywhere), it is moral rules that he has in mind when he formulates his theory of 'critical conventionalism' or 'duality of facts and norms'. Too often conventional moral rules have been presented as if they are beyond human interference in the same way as physical regularities are. I quite agree with Popper when he says that these rules are man-made and can be altered by human beings deciding not to observe them any more. But what are called moral principles differ from moral rules in this, that there is an element of naturalness about them. That is to say, moral principles embody general conceptions which, as against whatever opposes them, are acceptable to a human being when the matter is looked at from a rational point of view.

Hare in his book *The Language of Morals* seems to be advocating a kind of decision theory. In his book a great deal of emphasis is placed on the question of moral education and rightly so. He seeks to show that moral conduct is not a process of deduction from self-evident principles, but a process of deciding on principles themselves. A moral education which teaches people to follow principles blindly and not take individual decisions is therefore faulty. Hare takes an artificial example of a man who can know by a peculiar kind of clairvoyance everything about the effects of all the alternative actions open to him, but he does not yet possess any principles of conduct. If such a man decides between two alternative courses of actions and we ask him 'Why did you choose this set of effects rather than that?' his answer may be of two kinds. He might say, 'I can't give any reasons, I just felt like deciding that way.' On the other hand, he may say, 'It was this and this that made me decide. I was deliberately avoiding such and such effects, and seeking such and such.' If the man gave the second kind of answer he has started to form principles for himself. This shows that a principle need not be there before one acts. Also one need not adopt a principle permanently because one acts on it on some occasion. It is not that Hare belittles the function of principles in our decisions. He argues that without principles we could not learn anything whatsoever from our elders. But he believes that it is not good for us to be taught some principles allegedly self-evident like 'tell the truth'. For whether we should tell the truth or not depends on the situation in which we are to say something or other. There is no principle that is self-evident in the sense that it releases us from the responsibility of taking our own decisions. In fact, our decisions are decisions of principles which, far from being self-evident, take shape through our acts of choice. This I believe is very acceptable as far as it goes, but I do not think that it goes far enough. No doubt it is not enough for us to know some principles by heart, we must learn to take decisions, and to take decisions is sometimes to form principles for ourselves which we were never taught. Yet a principle which we arrive at by a process of independent choice is worth its name not because of the fact that we have decided on it but because it is fitting to the moral situation. A principle like 'it is better not to tell the truth when it causes more mischief than good' may in a certain sense be said to be formed by us if we were just taught 'tell the truth'. But this modified principle as well as the unqualified one are both implied in the still higher principle, 'treat every man as an end in himself'. And this principle, whatever the case with other principles may appear to be, is not so much the effect of any moral decision as its cause, whether or not it is consciously before our minds in any act of choice and whether or not we possess any verbal knowledge of it whatsoever.

Hare recognizes that there is a certain sense in which some moral principles are there already independently of our decisions. But he decides to give sociological and psychological explanations of such principles rather than explore their character from a value point of view. 'In a sense it is indeed there already if our fathers and grandfathers for unnumbered generations have all agreed in subscribing to it, and no one can break it without a feeling of compunction bred in him by years of education. If everyone would agree—with complete conviction—that a certain kind of act ought not to be done, then in saying that it ought not to be done I do indeed speak with an authority which is not my own. And my knowledge that I speak with authority—that I do not need to do more than subscribe to a principle that is already well established—is in a sense a knowledge of fact.'[1] But this sense is not such that principles gain a status independent of our decisions. Hare continues: 'But we must, nevertheless, carefully distinguish between two elements in the judgment. That the principle is well established (i.e. that everyone would agree with it) and that I have feelings of compunction if I break it, are facts; but when I subscribe to the principle, I do not state a fact, but make a moral decision.'[2] No doubt I do but it may still be asked what about the principle itself? When I subscribe to a principle I take a decision, but whence comes the authority of the principle itself? To say that it has authority because my forefathers have subscribed to it and because it has been bred in me by years of education, is to reduce morality to sociology; to say because I cannot break it without compunction is to reduce it to psychology.

A principle is, of course, not a principle unless one can decide to act on it and the responsibility for the decision rests on the individual himself. Yet surely a moral decision does not create a principle (except in the sense in which a value-fact would not exist unless it was valued) but recognizes one. It is not being suggested that principles have an ideal existence in a different kind of reality behind the scenes. Their existence is nothing but the regulative authority they have over our moral choice; and

---

[1] *The Language of Morals*, pp. 195–6.   [2] Ibid., p. 196.

this regulative authority is not constituted of our decisions, rather our decisions when morally suitable imply such authority. To understand morality, so it seems to me, is really to understand why, as Hare puts it, everyone would agree that a certain kind of act ought not to be done. And such understanding can only come from the realization that the principle involved in the undertaking of such acts rather than its opposite expresses some facts which a rational being, looking at human conduct from a value point of view, cannot but take cognizance of.

Another thinker who exalts moral practice at the cost of theoretical understanding of morals is Nowell-Smith. The concern of moral philosophy, says Nowell-Smith, is with concepts that we use in practical discourse—in deciding, choosing, advising, appraising, praising and blaming. What we want to know from Ethics is how to live our lives, not what things are. It is, therefore, a mistake to treat moral concepts, as they used to be treated of old, as if they are concerned with the knowledge of theoretical truths.

Let us try to see why Nowell-Smith thinks that moral concepts have no theoretical reference. The function of the concept 'ought' is to express decisions while 'right' and 'good' give reasons for such decisions. 'The difference between "right" and "ought" is, roughly, that while "I ought" and "you ought" are used to express decisions and injunctions, "right" is mainly used to support decisions and injunctions in a special way . . .'[1] To use the word 'right' in connection with an action that has been decided upon, for example, is to imply that the action conforms to a rule. 'But the mere existence of a rule is not a (logically) good reason for anybody's doing anything; and if the function of "right" was simply to promulgate or draw attention to a rule without implying a pro-attitude towards obeying it, it could not be used to give logically impeccable reasons for choosing and advising.'[2] To use a moral concept thus is to imply a pro-attitude, and it is this that differentiates a moral concept from a theoretical one.

I would agree that a pro-attitude is implied in a moral discourse. But it is not at all clear to me that this consideration needs make

[1] *Ethics*, pp. 185–6.   [2] Ibid., p. 188.

us say that the standards and rules implied in the use of 'good' and 'right' cannot be thought of as appropriate issues of theoretical understanding as well—so long as 'theoretical' is not defined so narrowly as to make everything else but issues that are technically scientific non-theoretical.

To continue with Nowell-Smith. Since the function of moral concepts is to help one to perform activities like deciding, choosing, etc., which is different from the function of expressing theoretical truths, judgments like 'You ought to do X' and 'I ought not' do not contradict each other. 'If Jones says to Smith "You ought to do X" and Smith replies "No, I ought not", are they contradicting each other? Must we say that the one is necessarily correct and the other mistaken? We have seen that sentences used for registering decisions or giving advice contextually imply certain causal and predictive elements which are indeed true or false; so that if the dispute between Smith and Jones is found to be concerned with any of these elements, they are contradicting each other and one of them must be mistaken. Among these elements in the case of ought sentences would be the existence of a rule recognized by both parties or a command issued by an authority whom they both recognize.'[1] 'But it is impossible that elements of this kind should be the sole elements in the use of ought sentences. If they were it would be impossible to understand the role that these sentences play in deciding, advising, preaching and exhorting. For the first of these activities it is necessary that Smith should have a pro-attitude towards doing what he thinks he ought to do; otherwise "I ought" is irrelevant to his problem of choice.'[2] Further, 'Now it is true that in ordinary life we should say that Smith and Jones were contradicting each other. But this only illustrates the danger of drawing philosophical conclusions from ordinary language. "Contradicting", which literally means "speaking against", can be used of almost any kind of verbal disagreement; but it also has a technical logician's use which was designed to elucidate empirical discourse. And if we speak of conflicting moral attitudes as "contradictory" we run the risk of unconsciously assimilating moral

[1] *Ethics*, pp. 193–4.   [2] Ibid., p. 194.

disputes to empirical ones and of inventing in the logic of moral discourse elements analogous to those which are bound up with the notion of contradiction in empirical discourse. One of these is "correspondence with the facts". And this is to court disaster.'[1]

It is no doubt true that the logic of moral discourse and the logic of what is called 'empirical discourse' are not entirely the same; for a moral discourse involves certain conceptions of value which an empirical discourse does not. But once we have understood a piece of reasoning to be moral reasoning—reasoning which is supposed to be in accordance with certain standards of value—it becomes possible for two people to contradict each other in the logical sense of the term 'contradiction' and not merely in the sense of speaking against; although I do not wish to say that every case of opposition in moral discourse is necessarily a case of logical contradiction. Of course, if the notion of 'contradiction' is conceived to be necessarily bound up with the notion of 'correspondence with facts' then there can be no contradiction in moral discourse, since the only facts with which anything can correspond are descriptive facts, and moral issues are not descriptive facts. But in any case there is moral opposition, and this opposition can be of a logical character, so long as we understand the logic to be the logic of moral reasoning.

Moral judgments are, says Nowell-Smith, expressions of decisions and not of theoretical truths. True enough, if we confine our attention to practical judgments like, 'I ought to do X', but general moral judgments like, 'the truth ought to be told' are expressions not of particular decisions to do anything but of what we may call 'moral truths', and these may be referred to as theoretical in some sense in spite of their practical implications.

PART 2. THE ATTITUDE THEORY OF MORALS

I shall here discuss the Attitude Theory of Morals as advocated by Stevenson in his *Ethics and Language*. Moral disagreement, says Stevenson, may be a matter of disagreement of belief or of attitude or both, but it is disagreement in attitude which is

---

[1] *Ethics*, p. 195.

ethically most significant. Disagreement in belief may be resolved by means of factual enquiry; not so disagreement in attitude which exists in spite of agreement on facts. A normative judgment on an issue is rooted in some attitude or other towards it. It is therefore important to understand that if an ethical agreement cannot be produced by producing agreement on all relevant factual matters it is a case of disagreement in attitude which cannot be solved in the way in which a purely factual dispute like 'When was Jones last in to tea?' can be.

Now Stevenson does not say that ethical disagreement is a case of disagreement in attitude and leave it at that. It is possible and necessary to redirect attitudes, particularly attitudes that are involved in ethical judgments. But if a disagreement is fundamentally a disagreement in attitude (i.e. a case where relevant beliefs held by both the parties are the same) the method employed has to be persuasive rather than rational (i.e. a method in which the disputants advance certain facts believing that a consideration of these will make the person in opposition think differently). The terms by using which we try to change or redirect people's attitudes are normative terms like 'good' and 'right' which work on them, according to Stevenson, through suggestions of emotive and imperative nature. Thus to say 'X is good' is to say 'I approve of X, do so as well'. When we use such terms we do not give anybody any additional information about the issue in question, but express our attitudes of approval or disapproval towards it and appeal to others to feel the same as we do. No doubt it is possible for us to give reasons why we consider that X is good and they are of the nature 'X has relations and consequences P, Q, R'. But if an existing attitude on X has been formed—as is not impossible—in spite of the knowledge that it has relations or consequences P, Q, R, then the advancing of the reason 'X has relations or consequences P, Q, R' will not change the attitude in question. There is no logical connection between a set of beliefs and an attitude, the connection is psychological. Two people may be aware that X has relations or consequences P, Q, R, and yet have different attitudes towards it on this very account, one approving of it and another disapproving.

G

The methods for solving ethical disputes are then two-fold. The ordinary rational method of advancing factual reasons where disagreement is rooted in someone's ignorance of such reasons, and the persuasive method for cases which show disagreement in attitude and not in belief; and this latter method works through emotional appeal and imperative suggestion. Ethical terms like 'right' and 'good', through employing which such appeal is made, may then be said to be emotive and imperative in nature. That is to say, when we wish to redirect other people's attitude to X, X being something that we value and they do not, we express our own emotion of approval towards it and suggest that the hearers may do the same and our expressions and suggestions may be expected to arouse a range of feelings in the hearers which would facilitate their coming to have the same attitude towards X as we have.

I believe that Stevenson is right in saying that many of our moral disagreements are disagreements in attitude and that such disagreements can be resolved only through a redirection of attitudes and not merely by producing factual evidence. I would also agree that in most cases attitudes can be redirected, if they can be redirected at all, by an appeal to the emotions; for although I believe that ethical issues are in some sense rational, our thinking upon them is initiated by our being emotionally moved by such issues. It is unlikely that an attitude towards an issue or object can be changed without there being produced an appropriate emotional orientation towards it. But I do not find Stevenson's theory acceptable in so far as he suggests: (a) that producing an emotional orientation towards an issue (i.e. a pro-attitude) is merely a matter of appealing to feelings; (b) that the meaning of ethical terms is emotive; (c) that the relation between a set of beliefs and an ethical attitude can only be psychological and never logical; and (d) that ethical judgments cannot significantly be called 'valid' or 'true'. Let us now turn to a consideration of these questions.

(a) A and B have a difference of attitude (as bereft of all differences in factual beliefs) towards X. B says 'X is bad', which means that he has an emotion of disapproval towards X. A approves of X and wishing to produce the same emotion in B towards X he says, 'X is good', and the use of the word 'good' here will, according to Stevenson, accomplish this by arousing a range of feelings in B. This account seems to me to be inadequate in two ways. First, we cannot say categorically that the use of the word 'good' produces a range of feelings in the hearer, for it might leave him totally unmoved. All that can be said is that to use the word 'good' is to suggest to the hearer that he should change his feelings. Secondly, we can hardly expect all Bs to be so naïve as to change their existing feelings towards X merely because a word has been used which suggests that they should change their feelings. Moreover human emotions or attitudes[1] are much more complex than feelings, as they involve tendencies to think and act as well. We may come to favour something emotionally because it arouses our feelings; this may happen, equally, through our coming to think of the object or issue in a new light which helps to arouse our feelings. It is much more plausible that B's attitude can be changed—if B does have a fundamental disagreement of attitude with A—through A helping him to look at the issue from a point of view different from what he has hitherto adopted than that it can be changed merely by suggesting that he should change his feelings. And although one cannot be made to adopt a different point of view by means of what is ordinarily called 'arguments', it certainly involves persuasive processes that are in some ways rational and not merely emotional. For instance, B, who belongs to a higher caste, may be refusing to let P, who is an 'untouchable', enter a temple. A might try to persuade B by saying that P is also a human being with the same sort of feelings and needs as people who belong to upper castes and his act of refusal is really a refusal to treat him as a human being. Now B, whose attitude towards the question has been conditioned by tradition, may never have thought of it in this light and what A has said might lead him to feel differently about the issue. But A appealed not merely

---

[1] One of the differences between 'emotion' and 'attitude' is this. When we talk about attitudes we talk about tendencies that are relatively permanent, there may not be any suggestion of permanence when we talk about emotions.

to his feeling but to his capacity to think or reason as well (and this use of reason involves more than a consideration of factual evidence).

(*b*) It appears to me that the meaning of ethical terms like 'right', 'good', 'justice', 'honest', etc., do have referents of a certain sort and by this I mean something more than what has been called their 'descriptive meaning'. The descriptive meaning of the term 'good' in the sentence 'she is a good girl' uttered by a particular person in a certain context may be 'she goes to church on Sundays'. It might be something quite different when uttered in a different context. What I wish to say when I say ethical terms have referents is this. A moral point of view is a characteristic point of view and to value or disvalue something morally is to look at it in a distinctive way. In so far as a moral point of view is an evaluative point of view whose ultimate standard of judgment is the requirement that individual human beings should behave in such a way as to be as happy as it is in their nature to be and as to let others be happy in the same way as well, moral terms, when used consistently, imply that the objects referred to by them are characterized by being not inconsistent with the requirement of morality. In short, moral terms express and evoke emotions, suggest the undertaking of certain actions and so on and at the same time imply that the issues in respect of which they can be applied are characterized in a certain way which distinguishes them from issues of an opposite character.

That the use of the term 'good' expresses something more than feeling is recognized by Stevenson himself. For he agrees that 'this is good' is more nearly approximated in its full meaning by 'this is worthy of approval'. Now if what one approves of is also worthy of approval—the reason why the speaker would recommend its acceptance by the hearer—it must have some characteristics, however vaguely and imperfectly understood, by virtue of which it is to be differentiated from what is not worthy of approval; and this cannot be the mere fact that the object arouses the emotion of approval. What is worthy of approval does not necessarily produce the emotion of approval nor is the emotion of approval restricted exclusively to what is worthy of approval. Stevenson can no doubt defend his position by saying that 'X is worthy of approval' means only that other people have an attitude of approval towards it, and it is this that is being approved and not any quality or characteristic of X. But this is not how the word 'worthy' functions in ordinary speech. 'Worthy' means 'having worth' and by 'worth' is meant—so says the dictionary—'that quality or characteristic of a thing which renders it valuable or useful'. Stevenson might, of course, wish to give a technical meaning to it, but even so, his account does not appear to be very satisfactory. If when someone says 'X is good', he is not simply expressing an attitude of approval towards X but is expressing an attitude of approval towards other people's attitude of approval towards X, then his attitude towards X (not his attitude towards others' attitude to X) is not a purely personal attitude but has an impersonal or objective element in it in so far as a great many people agree in having the same attitude towards it. It may then be said that X has some distinguishable features on account of which people come to have an attitude of approval towards it. No doubt Stevenson might say that the fact that other people have an attitude of approval towards X is an accident and does not signify anything objective about it. But if it is possible for us to indicate the sort of objective features that an object or issue which is called 'good' in a moral context may have, then it is more reasonable, so it seems to me, to think—when people agree in saying that X is good—that X has features approachable in common between them than to think that it is purely an accident that they agree.

(*c*) Let us now discuss if the relation between an ethical attitude and a certain set of factual beliefs is purely psychological and never logical. If by saying that this relation is psychological Stevenson means that certain ethical issues are so highly complex that it is possible for different people to have different attitudes towards them even when all their factual aspects have been fully explored—without anyone being necessarily guilty of unreasonableness—then I quite agree. But Stevenson says more than that, he says that this relation can only be psychological and never logical. Closely related to this question are the questions of the rationality and validity of ethical arguments and I shall discuss these all together.

If any ethical dispute, says Stevenson, is rooted in disagreement in belief, it may be settled by reasoning and enquiry to whatever extent the beliefs may be so settled. But if an ethical dispute is not rooted in disagreement in belief no reasonable solution of any sort is possible. The supporting reasons in morals have only to do with beliefs, they are related to the judgment neither inductively nor deductively and the connection between them is psychological rather than logical. Now the relation between a set of reasons R and an ethical conclusion E being neither inductive nor deductive, Stevenson suggests that we should cease to talk about a moral argument being valid or true; for if we do not do so, we are claiming that there is a special kind of validity or truth which pertains to Ethics and there is no warrant for this claim. The reasons advanced in course of an ethical argument support the judgment in the way that reasons support imperatives. Imperatives are not true or false, nor are ethical conclusions.

Now when Stevenson is denying that reasons given in favour of an attitude can have any logical compulsion, he is using the term 'logical' in a limited sense—in the sense of processes that are involved in inductive or deductive argumentation. He believes that the reasons given have some sort of force, they support or back up an ethical judgment in such a way as to make it acceptable to the hearer. Now if this is to happen irrespective of who the speaker or hearer is, it does not seem to me to be quite correct to consider the necessity involved in this process as purely psychological and not logical. Clearly, as Stevenson himself points out, the step from factual reason to ethical conclusion cannot be either inductively or demonstratively valid. Moral reasoning, as apart from moral reflection, is like this; X is good because (supposing that it is not immediately accepted) X means P and the absence of X means not-P, and P is a sort of thing which a reasonable person cannot fail to find preferable to not-P, if he is to compare the two seriously. Here the conclusion 'X is good' follows from 'X means P' according to the logic which entitles us to accept 'P is a sort of thing which no reasonable person, etc.' as an appropriate standard of evaluation in the matter. When I say it follows I mean this. If we accept that P is the sort of thing, etc., and that X means P, we do not find the judgment 'X is bad' a tenable (and in that sense valid) judgment. The term 'validity' does certainly have a truth-claim as Stevenson says. But unless the term 'true' is used as synonymous with 'verifiable through sense experience' there is no reason why we cannot say that a piece of moral reasoning is valid or otherwise without having to claim that validity in Ethics is of a special kind. Of course, a piece of moral reasoning is quite often not so simple or straightforward and there are cases where we do not know which conclusion to draw from a given set of standards and facts. There are also cases where no evaluative judgment has as yet taken shape and we are perplexed as to how exactly to assess the thing or the situation, for there seems to be more than one standard involved or the standard involved may be so general and the situation so complex that nothing very conclusive follows. What I am contesting is the general theory that the notion of 'validity' does not apply to moral reasoning.

Now as to the relation between a set of factual reasons and an ethical attitude. If by saying that this relation is psychological is meant that some moral situations are such that no one attitude seems to be the only attitude that fits the facts present, then, of course, it is true. But there are other situations in which we do not doubt that a particular attitude (or type of attitude) fits the facts present as against an attitude of an opposite character, if, of course, we look at the facts from a distinctive point of view, namely, that of morality. In such cases, then, it will be reasonable, according to the logic of moral reasoning, to hold such an attitude and unreasonable to hold an attitude of an opposite character. Now the logic of moral reasoning, as we have already noticed, is not inductive or deductive in process. But there is no reason why the term 'logic' should be restricted to induction or deduction. The term 'logic' or 'logical' is also used to signify any necessity that we find to be involved in any process of thought. And in so far as there is a place for reason in ethical deliberations and in the moulding of attitudes, and in so far as reasons given may establish a judgment or an attitude or fail to do so, it seems to be quite in keeping with common usage to say that a process of moral reasoning may either possess or lack logical force. This force is referred to by such remarks as that one is being reasonable or unreasonable in one's attitude or judgment. We hear of such expressions as the 'logic of words' or the 'logic of language' where the word 'logic' has no association with induction or deduction. When we talk about the logic of a word we have some such thing in mind as the way in which—it may reasonably be supposed—a symbol functions in our thought and speech, or the way in which a symbol fits in with the conceptions of things it may reasonably be used to describe or refer to. Now a symbol may function in more than one way, some of which are not consistent with one another. But it is only reasonable to suppose that a symbol would have some sort of fixed reference within a certain context of thought, as otherwise any interchange of thought would not be possible. By the logic of a word, then, we mean the consistent functioning of a word that fits in within a certain context of thought. Thus it appears to be perfectly justifiable to talk about the logic of moral reasoning and thinking where the word 'logic' implies the necessity that is involved in this that certain conceptions and not others are acceptable as suitable standards of moral evaluation. Moral attitudes, then, can be logical or not, according as they fit the facts or not when looked at from the moral point of view.

What Stevenson is up against, however, is not so much the function of logic in moral reasoning and reflection as such, as the kind of logic which is thought to be the characteristic of the so-called 'Cartesian system' in morals. The Cartesian system is said to uphold that there are some general moral principles and ends from which it is possible to deduce the particular moral rules that should be prevalent in human societies irrespective of any considerations of the special circumstances to be found in particular societies. There can therefore be only one moral code binding upon all. This Stevenson, as so many other thinkers, would reject and it seems that the attitude theory is an escape from this method. If what are right and good are matters of our attitudes which are emotive in nature and not the outcome of any rational process, then there has not got to be the same system of moral code for all of us. But perhaps the so-called 'Cartesian system' admits of a different interpretation. It is not that there is only one moral code which is binding on all human societies and which is to be deduced from the conceptions of some ends and principles self-evident to all. Rather, we may begin our moral reflection with the fact that differing moral codes exist, but try to understand the satisfactoriness or otherwise of such codes or aspects of such codes by looking upon them as the working out of certain worthwhile ends and principles under specific circumstances of life. The question therefore is not 'What rules and specific ways of behaving can we deduce from these ends and principles that will be valid in any society at any time?' but 'Is there any reason to think that the rules or the specific ways of behaving that are approved of in this society are not in accordance with the conceptions of ends and principles that have self-evident validity, *considering that certain circumstances are what they are*?' This is not a simple question, nor is there a straightforward answer to it. But it is an intelligible question, as moral assessment of codes or aspects of codes are frequently being made in terms of standards that are somehow accepted as beyond question, which the aspects being judged are not considered to be.

Stevenson accuses the traditional writers on Ethics of placing too much emphasis on the component of belief in ethical agreement and disagreement and too little on attitudes. The reason why the traditional writers have devoted their attention to what Stevenson calls the 'cognitive aspects' of the matter is not far to seek. The direct aim of philosophers, as distinct from that of practical moral reformers, is not to urge people to any particular course of action (which, of course, they may do) but to clarify the implications of the conceptions in terms of which moral approach to facts is to be guided. And these implications are to be understood in relation to experiences of a characteristic nature with which these conceptions are found to fit in. Emotional factors are undoubtedly involved in any moral approach to facts, and they exert a considerable influence on the course that moral actions may take. But if what we are seeking is a clearer understanding of what is involved in the point of view of morality we shall not be satisfied merely by being told that moral issues arouse the emotions of approval and disapproval. We also want to know why is it that we approve of certain things and disapprove of others, and what are the standards, acceptable by all from a rational point of view, by which we judge certain things as worthy of moral approval. Hence the importance of belief or cognition in a philosophical treatment of Ethics. Moreover to have an attitude is not just to have a range of feelings towards some issue; it is also to think and act in characteristic ways in respect of this issue. Had Stevenson himself not placed an exaggerated emphasis on emotional factors and had he broadened his conception of 'attitude' to include not only emotions but also ways of thinking and acting, he would perhaps have found that the traditional philosophical approach to Ethics has also its value.

PART 3.　THE COMMAND THEORY OF MORALS

The command theory of morals originates with the realization that ethical sentences are closely bound up with our actions in a way in which purely descriptive sentences are not. In a sentence like 'the colour of the dress she wore last night is green' our object is to describe a particular state of affairs which is easily identifiable as such from amongst various other similarly describable states of affairs that have taken place or may take place. In an ethical judgment like 'you should tell the truth' we are concerned not with descriptions of things that have happened or may happen but with judging that conduct of a certain kind (truth-telling) rather than another (telling lies) is preferable in human speech. Ethical judgments are of various kinds and these are concerned with the particular actions that we should perform, the principles by which we should choose the action to be performed from amongst various possible ones, and the kind of persons we should be so that the particular actions we perform and the principles by which we choose them are of the desirable kind. The peculiar concern of ethical judgments is then with human actions as approached, of course, in a characteristic manner, and it is amongst their functions to tell us that we should do certain sorts of things and refrain from others.

But the question which is philosophically important in this connection is this: 'Can we explain the characteristic nature of morality by reference to the fact that the function of a moral judgment is to tell us to do something?' Or is it that the judgment tells us to do something because what it tells us to do under a specific circumstance is in accordance with a value ideal (or ideals) of human conduct? If so, to say simply that moral judgments are imperative sentences or commands the function of which is to make us do certain things is not to offer an adequate explanation of moral conceptions. For moral conceptions not only tell us to do certain things, their function is also to explain how certain things which we think we should do are worthwhile for us to undertake.

Ethical statements, says Prof. Ayer, are not statements which can in the literal sense be considered to be significant, for it is not their job to describe any fact. Their job is to express the speaker's emotions and to arouse feelings and stimulate actions. Indeed some of them are used in such a way as to give the sentences in which they occur the effect of commands. Now it is not to be denied that certain ethical sentences are used purely as commands nor that all ethical sentences have an aspect which may be looked upon as a command. But it is doubtful whether to say that the sentence 'it is your duty to tell the truth' expresses a certain sort of ethical feeling and commands one to tell the truth is to explain all that is involved in it. For one might ask 'Is this feeling that is being expressed a feeling that is suitable in a moral context?' or 'Is this command one that is morally defensible?' Suppose that the sentence was 'you should not tell him the truth, he would not know about it unless you told him, and the money would be yours'. This no doubt expresses a feeling and a command. But is this feeling a morally defensible feeling and the command one that, ethically speaking, compels obedience? This can hardly be maintained. Moral feelings and commands are, at any rate, a very special sort of feelings and commands, and to understand how they differ from other feelings and commands is to understand how they are suitable in a particular context that is moral.

In fact whether we should say that a sentence in the imperative mood is to be called a command or not depends upon the point of view from which it is uttered. Let us take, for example, a particular sentence, 'you should pay your fare even if the conductor forgets to ask for it', which may be a piece of advice given by a father to his son. This sentence is different from the sentence which a conductor might utter when a passenger is trying to get off the bus without paying, 'you should pay your fare'. The difference lies in this. The father's advice to the son might be given even when a situation of non-payment has not actually arisen or even if there is no definite reason to think that the son is planning to have a ride without payment, while the conductor can say this to a passenger only if there is reason to think that he intends to avoid payment. The conductor's imperative is directly aimed at making the man pay his fare apart from its being an expression of indignation at his not having done so. The father's statement is, of course, also aimed at making the son act in a certain way, yet it can hardly be a direct command to the son to pay his fare there and then—in the way the conductor's statement is a command to the passenger if the situation is not such that the question of paying the fare is immediately relevant. The father's statement is more a suggestion than an order, a suggestion about the desirability of the son's behaving in one way rather than another even when he has a free choice to do either, although it is also expected that the suggestion will lead to the son's behaving in the way that is desirable. The passenger who is trying to avoid payment cannot come out with 'Why should I?'—the mere fact that the conductor is asking for the fare rules this out. (We can overlook exceptional cases for our present purposes.) But the son may (although it is not very likely that he would) ask 'Why should I pay the fare if I have a chance to get away?' which would show that paying the fare when the conductor asks for it and paying it even when the conductor forgets to do so are not identical actions. The answer to this question may be of two kinds. (1) The father might say, 'Although the conductor might have forgotten, an inspector might suddenly appear and check just as you are trying to get off and that would mean trouble for you.' (2) He might say, 'It is only reasonable that one should recognize services received and be willing to return the benefit in the acknowledged form. You pay back in the form of fares the advantage you derive from the fact that a bus service is run by the State or other proprietor. You would not like anyone to take advantage of you, why should you want to take advantage of the bus service and not be willing to pay for it.' Answer (1), we would say, is from the point of view of prudence while answer (2) is from the point of view of what is desirable and reasonable for its own sake and is therefore an instance of moral reasoning proper. Every moral judgment of an imperative form, we can see from above, is then not a mere command, for it can also involve an assertion that what is being commanded is reasonable when looked at from the point of view of what is best for its own sake for beings who are human. A moral command (which is a command in an extended sense and is not the sort of command which anyone could issue to others on the strength of his superior position in some way) then has authority not primarily because it is backed by power but because it recommends itself to a rational approach to the question 'What sort of behaviour on the part of human beings is desirable for its own sake?' If the son cannot reject his father's advice, suggestion, or command, it is because he somehow recognizes that it is better to acknowledge advantages and benefits received than not to do so. It is only because of this recognition that he will be ready to pay his fare even when the conductor forgets to ask for it, and when he can be practically certain that there is no possibility of an inspector appearing before he has a chance to get off the bus. The authority of the command, if we call it a command, that the father has issued then comes not so much from the fact that the father has a superior status or power by virtue of which it can be expected that the son will obey his wishes, as from the fact that the son will have no difficulty, if the question is approached rationally, in telling himself to do what the father has told him to do. I have no wish to suggest that every authority that is backed by power is devoid of rational appeal. But the fact that it is backed by power and the fact that it appeals to a rational approach are distinguishable facts; and an authority backed by power may continue to issue commands even when it has not got, or has lost, rational appeal. If we understand what it means to say that the authority of moral judgments lies in their rational appeal, it can hardly be maintained, as Ayer does in *Language, Truth and Logic*, that moral precepts have for some people the force of commands because of the sanction of society behind them or because of the fear of God's displeasure.

According to Prof. Ayer, moral judgments of whatever form they may be, 'it is your duty to tell the truth', 'one ought to tell the truth', 'it is good to tell the truth', can all be explained by saying that they are commands calculated to provoke certain actions in us, the difference being in the tone of emphasis put on the command. But a statement of the form 'it is your duty to tell the truth' is usually made in an occasion of a particular nature when someone has to say something, or when someone may do so, and what one says may either be the truth or not. 'You (in the sense of one) ought to tell the truth' is more of a general statement which may be made even when the question of saying something is not immediately relevant. Also, this general statement is compatible with a statement like 'you should not tell him, at the present stage of his illness, that his best friend has died; the shock might be too much for him to bear'. The general statement, then, can be called a command only in an indirect way; and the difference between this statement and the particular one 'it is your duty to tell the truth' (now, in this case) cannot be explained by the tone of emphasis. One may be as emphatic about the general statement as about the particular one. The difference lies in *what* they tell us, not merely in what tone of voice and with what feeling they tell us to do a certain thing. The general statement no doubt has the practical object in view of influencing us in favour of telling the truth as against not doing so. But it is no less its function to make this implicit assertion that telling the truth is preferable, from the point of view of morality, to telling lies in so far as not to tell the truth is to violate the value that an individual's desire to know has for its own sake. If this is acceptable, it can hardly be said that sentences which simply express moral judgments do not say anything.

Hare in his book *The Language of Morals* criticizes the simpler type of the command theory as advanced by Carnap and Ayer. He contests the idea that the function of a command is to get the hearer to do something. He advocates that it is simply to tell someone what he is to do. What then is the difference between an ethical sentence and an ordinary sentence of the form 'S is P'? The language of morals, says Hare, is one sort of prescriptive language, while a sentence of the form 'S is P' is descriptive. Prescriptive language is the language which prescribes a course of action for us rather than describes a state of affairs and it includes value judgments amongst which are moral ones, as well as the different kinds of imperatives which may be covered by the single term 'command'. A moral judgment differs from an ordinary imperative by virtue of the fact that it employs terms like 'right', 'good' and 'ought' which have an evaluative or commendatory function (i.e. they recommend something to our choice in a context in which some decision has to be arrived at and an action undertaken). Leaving this aspect aside, it has many features in common with an ordinary imperative sentence. We can therefore attempt an understanding of value judgments through an understanding of imperatives.

A typical indicative sentence is a statement. It is used for telling someone that something is the case, an imperative is used to tell someone to make something the case. An imperative sentence cannot be reduced to the indicative. That does not mean, of course, that only indicative sentences are significant and imperatives merely express wishes. The indicative sentence 'you are going to shut the door' is different from the imperative sentence 'shut the door'. Yet both are about the same thing, 'your shutting the door in the immediate future', which is a recognizable state of affairs actual or possible. Only what is done with this is different in indicative and imperative sentences.

If this is the case it is difficult to see why Hare should believe, as he does, that moral judgments do not state any fact at all. If we were to rewrite the moral imperative, 'tell the truth', into phrastic and neustic (a device used by Hare) it would read like 'your telling the truth in the immediate future, please', and the corresponding indicative, 'you are going to tell the truth', may be written as, 'your telling the truth in the immediate future, yes'. The phrastic in these two sentences, 'your telling the truth', must stand for a recognizable state of affairs in much the same way as 'your shutting the door' does, and this is being referred to in both the sentences, although in different ways. It may then be said that the function of the conception of 'telling the truth' is to state a recognizable aspect of our experience and, as I have already maintained, it is quite in keeping with common usage to refer to such aspects as facts. As for the hearer, to nod assent to an indicative sentence, says Hare, means (if he is sincere) that he believes the statement to be true, while to nod assent to an imperative one is to do what the imperative tells one to do. One cannot say 'yes, sir' to the imperative 'shut the door' and yet not do it. To assent to the moral imperative 'tell the truth' is actually to tell the truth when a relevant situation arises. But it seems to me quite possible for someone to accept 'tell the truth' as a tenable moral judgment (which is giving assent to it in some way) and yet not tell the truth when an occasion arises for doing so even if it is not impossible for him to do so for physiological and psychological reasons (except when 'psychological reasons' is so defined that it is not possible for an individual to do anything but what he does). 'Tell the truth' cannot in such a case mean a second person command (which it sometimes is) but is a general statement to the effect that truth-telling is a characteristic of human speech which is preferable to its absence or opposite. This, of course, cannot be called a descriptive sentence as ordinarily understood. Yet I do not see any reason why this cannot be called an indicative sentence in so far as this indicates or asserts a case, however important a bearing it may have on our actions. Indeed, it seems to make little difference to our understanding of the fact that the action of truth-telling is morally desirable, whether this is formulated in the form of an indicative or an imperative sentence. I have no wish to deny the distinction that there is between an indicative and an imperative sentence. Only the understanding of this distinction does not seem to me to be the central point in the understanding of morals.

Hare, like Popper, wishes to say that a normative judgment belongs to a category which is utterly different from a statement of fact. To quote Popper from his article on 'What can Logic do for Philosophy?': 'Perhaps the simplest and the most important point about ethics is purely logical. I mean the impossibility to derive non-tautological, ethical rules—imperatives; principles of policy; aims; or however we may describe them—from states of fact.'[1] Says Hare, '... from a series of indicative sentences about "the character of any of its objects" no imperative sentence about what is to be done can be derived, and therefore no moral judgment can be derived from it either.'[2]

The point in these arguments appears to be the same as Moore was concerned with in his refutation of naturalism—that 'what ought to be' cannot be derived from 'what is'. But the point of the distinction that Moore makes between 'what is' and 'what ought to be' does not seem to me to correspond exactly either to the distinction between an indicative sentence and an imperative one or to the distinction between what is a statement of fact and what is not. 'What ought to be' is not the same as 'what is', yet 'what ought to be' may as well, in certain cases, be 'what is'. It is not only possible to say 'you ought to tell the truth', but also, 'I am pleased that you have told the truth'. This last statement indicates what a certain case is, but this is a moral judgment not by virtue of the fact that it indicates a certain state of affairs but because of the fact that the state of affairs is what it ought to be. But if 'what ought to be' can also be 'what is', even though these two conceptions are not the same, a statement containing a conception of 'what ought to be' may be considered to be an indicative sentence or a statement of fact in so far as such a statement would assert or indicate that something is the case. That is

[1] *Proceedings*, The Aristotelian Society, p. 154, Suppl. Vol., 1948.
[2] *The Language of Morals*, p. 30.

H

to say, there is a certain sense in which what is of value may be referred to as a fact, although a fact which is judged to be of value (what ought to be) is not the same as a fact which is not so judged (what simply is). Now, all this may seem very unimportant. What does it matter, one might say, whether a moral judgment is called an indicative or an imperative statement, a statement of fact or not a statement of fact, so long as we understand the distinction that there is between a moral judgment and a purely descriptive judgment like 'he is a very tall man'. The point, however, is an important one. For once we have called a moral judgment an imperative sentence (some moral judgments are no doubt imperatives; the point at issue is whether the name 'imperative' expresses the distinctive nature of what morality is concerned with), meaning thereby that what moral conceptions have to say cannot be said in an indicative form, we begin to think that moral statements are not statements of facts (only a fact can be asserted in an indicative sentence). And once we have accepted that moral statements are not statements of facts without making it quite clear that the term 'fact' is being used here in a limited sense (in the sense of a distinct object, quality or event, identifiable as such in different instances of its occurrence) we begin to believe that what moral judgments are concerned with are somehow matters of a different order than what is rationally approachable and defensible (i.e. fact in another sense of the term). From this it is an easy step to begin to believe that moral matters are matters of feelings, attitudes, decisions (not necessarily to be understood in terms of certain definite standards), social customs and so on. The effect is that it is no longer considered to be the case that there are fundamental moral distinctions which we know and talk about. Moral conceptions have importance, it is considered, from the point of view of our actions and emotions but not from the point of view of understanding a characteristic kind of our experience.

But the denial of the status of facts to moral conceptions has a deeper root than a purely grammatical one. Our judgments about facts which are distinct objects, qualities or events have a degree of certainty and such judgments are on the whole shared by different individuals. The things to which a moral conception like 'good' or 'right' may be applied by an individual or group of individuals may not be the same to which other individuals or groups would apply it and there is no formalized method by means of which the tenability of one opinion as against that of the other may be established in the same way as a conclusion about a fact (as defined above) may be. It seems natural to conclude from this that moral conceptions do not signify any fact, but as they are still important in respect of our actions, they stand for commands and for decisions which follow from these commands. But this is really no way out. For no command, except when it is backed by absolute and autocratic power, is devoid of all implications concerning certain states of affairs which make it desirable or at least necessary that the action should be undertaken.

Hare criticizes, by way of establishing his theory, the opinion which holds that moral conceptions stand for self-evident facts. The important points in Hare's arguments against self-evident principles may thus be summarized. First of all, a moral principle, if it is to be self-evident, must be analytic. An analytic proposition has no content, it cannot therefore tell us anything about our conduct. The principle which acts as the imperative major premise of our deductive moral reasoning must have content, otherwise we could not deduce the particular moral commands from it. It is, therefore, a synthetic proposition, which means that it is not self-evident. If we say that there is no imperative major premise in a piece of moral reasoning and we just pass from certain given facts (of the type 'S is false') to a conclusion (do not say S) by means of a special rule of moral inference (of the type 'one ought not to tell a lie') we create a certain logical difficulty. For a rule of inference being logical, it is a rule about correct thinking and talking and not about actions. How can we get a moral conclusion which does say something about our conduct (do not say S) merely out of a given fact (S is false) by the help of a logical rule which says nothing about conduct but merely deals with correct thinking?

If we examine ordinary moral opinion on this question, there appears nothing unusual about saying that the principle 'one ought to tell the truth' (understood as an abstract, general statement) cannot be rejected in so far as its rejection implies the acceptance of its contrary (similarly abstract and general) 'one ought to tell lies'. Does this mean that this principle is analytic? If by an analytic proposition we mean one that has no content in the sense that it cannot tell us anything about matters of fact, then the statement 'one ought to tell the truth' is clearly not analytic; for it does say something about our conduct. Nevertheless, the statement has no content in the sense that it is a formal statement from which no statement about particular actions follows deductively although particular actions may be judged from the point of view of morality to be suitable or unsuitable in a certain context in accordance with the conceptions that the statement involves. This statement is, of course, analytic in the sense that the conception of moral 'ought' involves the conception of 'telling the truth', so that it would be *self-contradictory from the point of view of morality* to say 'one ought to tell lies'. Yet it applies to matters of fact, because that to which it applies acquires the factual character it has from the point of view of morality, by being looked at through the conceptions that the statement involves. Kant endeavoured to explain the characteristic nature of such a statement by calling it 'synthetic (applies to experience) apriori' (not derived from experience, as it cannot be self-contradictory to reject anything that is derived purely from experience). It will perhaps be better, as the term 'apriori' is open to serious confusion, to call such a statement 'empirical (its function is to explain a certain feature of our experience) analytic' (cannot be made false through experience as it has already been conceived in such a way as to explain a feature of our experience, so long, of course, as we continue to experience this feature).

As to the question of moral inference. It seems perfectly natural to infer 'do not say S' from the given fact 'S is false'. We require the statement 'never say what is false' as an imperative major premise only if it has to be insisted upon that the nature of moral inference is deductive. If it can be accepted that a piece of moral reasoning may be other than deductive or inductive and yet not be inevitably loose, then there seems to be nothing against saying that one can infer 'do not say S' from the given fact S is false, on the strength of the moral standard 'one ought to tell the truth'. We may not call this standard a 'rule of inference' as ordinarily understood; yet it is like an inference-ticket or licence which justifies our passing from certain given facts (S is false) to a conclusion of a characteristic kind (do not say S) when we approach the matter in a certain way. Now, the function of this inference-ticket is a logical function, yet it does not follow that the standard is purely a rule about correct thinking, like the law of excluded middle, and does not say anything about our conduct at all. *For the logic here in question is the logic of moral reasoning,* and this being reasoning characterized by a certain approach to the objects of thought, the conceptions in terms of which we think appear also as the features of what is thought of. The logical nature of the standard 'the truth ought to be told' does not stop it from being factually informative or, as Hare puts it, from being a rule for behaving correctly.

Hare does, of course, say that moral conceptions have a commendatory function as well as an imperative one. But he does not go into the question as to what distinguishes moral commendation from any other kind of commendation to any serious extent. All he says is that the issues that are objects of moral commendation are of the nature of actions, and these are important for human beings. This no doubt is true, but it fails to point out the characteristic features of moral evaluation. For there are human actions, and important actions too, which are often commended from points of view other than the moral. What we want to know is why or by what standards we judge that certain issues or actions are objects specifically of moral commendation. To this the command theory, either the simpler variety or the more complex kind, supplies no answer.

CHAPTER V

The Characteristics of Moral Values

Now we come to a consideration of the distinctive point of view or approach to experience that we call morality and the characteristics of values which belong to this approach. To do this we shall have to see how moral values differ from non-value facts as well as from other possible values.

I am going to suggest that one of the distinctions between value (instrumental or intrinsic) and non-value facts lies in this, that whatever is, or is taken to be, a value implies the desirability of human happiness as against unhappiness, whereas whatever is simply stated as a fact (i.e. so long as its value is not being considered) does not necessarily imply this. I shall elaborate this point, in case it is not quite evident. But before I do so I would like to emphasize that what I have just said does not mean that the value of a thing is derived from the happiness it actually produces, for it may well be that a thing produces happiness because it is of value and not the other way round. Nevertheless, the valuation of a thing does imply the desirability of human happiness, and this holds true even though one may not value a thing because one thinks it will give him happiness. Now when we value a thing we may do so because it will help us to achieve something other than what is being directly aimed at, in which case it is called an instrumental value, or because of the thing itself, in which case it is called an intrinsic value. The same thing may, of course, be valued instrumentally or intrinsically, depending on the attitude one brings to bear on it. It is believed by most reflective people that there are certain things like knowledge, aesthetic qualities and moral goodness which ought to be valued intrinsically. For it is only when we value them intrinsically that we come to know their full significance as values which then appear to have a worth quite independent of any particular valuation (even though we know that they do not appear as values in a sub-human world) as distinct from anything valued instrumentally whose value—of this we become conscious on reflection—attaches to it because of the act of valuation. It seems to me that these, and not anything like material objects, money, power, glory, etc., are recommended for intrinsic valuation because of the quality they give to a life which knows their intrinsic value, as distinct from a life which can value them only instrumentally or which gives intrinsic value only to things like money, power, etc. It is hard to describe this quality, but it seems to me that a moment of realization of intrinsic value is a moment of that particular kind of happiness which is characterized by one's feeling fulfilled rather than gratified, a feeling of fulfilment in which there is no awareness of the satisfaction of a purely private purpose, and at the same time by one's being at peace with the universe (or, at any rate, by the absence of a feeling of conflict or disharmony). Such a moment is blissful rather than pleasurable.

We say that we ought to value things like knowledge, etc., because of their own intrinsic character. Yet the world will not be thought of as containing these values unless there were human beings (or any being capable of conceiving) to conceive of them as values. This shows, so it seems to me, that these values and their realization answer to some needs or calls felt by human beings (needs or calls which are conspicuous by their absence amongst non-human animals). To this the objection may be that if these things are valued because they answer to human needs their value is no longer intrinsic. This appears to me to be a misunderstanding as to the nature of intrinsic values. We are not saying that we ought to think of them as values because they satisfy human needs (this way of putting the matter suggests that they are not to be valued for their own sakes). Rather, to say that they are intrinsic values and to say that they answer to some calls felt by human beings are to approach the same thing from two different points of view. Their intrinsic character lies not in their being above any need felt by anyone but in their answering to a need of a special character which I have termed a 'call'. When we need money to buy food, money is an instrumental value, for the need for it is rooted in some other need. But when we feel a call to pursue knowledge because it is knowledge our need is self-creative and is not derived from something else. Of course, the need for food is not derived from something else either, but the need to pursue knowledge is different from it by not being present amongst non-human animals. Again, it is true that any-thing like the need to pursue money or power for its own sake is self-creative and peculiarly human. But it is distinct from the needs we are considering in so far as it, by its very nature, leads to conflict when pursued beyond a certain limit. In as much as the needs involved in the pursuit of intrinsic values do not do so, they may be called 'higher needs' or 'calls'. Now the intrinsic value of knowledge is not derived from someone pursuing it and its value is felt to be above any personal activity, but it implies that some humans at least feel a call to pursue it, for knowledge cannot be said to be a value in a sub-human world in which no being at all feels such a call. Whenever we value a thing instru-mentally or intrinsically, provided, of course, there is no reason why we should not value the things we do and our acts of valua-tion may be considered legitimate, we imply that the satisfaction of a human need (whether of the instinctive type felt more or less by all or the higher self-creative type which may be felt by some and not others) is desirable. And to consider this is to consider that human happiness which is consequent on such satisfaction is desirable and human unhappiness which arises out of lack of opportunity for such satisfaction is undesirable. This must not be construed as implying that knowledge is valuable as a means to happiness only. For in this context the conception of 'means and end' is not relevant. There are not two processes, pursuit of knowledge and when that is over, happiness. The pursuit of knowledge for its own sake, for one who values it, is happiness. A value is instrumental if the need for it is felt as the result of one's feeling some other need. There is no such thing as feeling a need for happiness. It is commonplace that one who consciously looks for happiness finds it the least, and whenever it is achieved it is achieved as a by-product of the attainment of some other value. Yet it may still be true that in recognizing the value, say of morality, one implicitly recognizes the value of happiness. But the term 'happiness' is ambiguous, and let us see how it is to be understood so that it may be taken as the implicate of all value points of view when the intrinsic ones are included amongst them.

By happiness may be meant pleasure or the feeling of gratification that is derived from the satisfaction of a personal desire without any implication as to the importance or strength of the desire in the totality of purposes in an individual's life. Pleasure may represent a value, it may not. Human beings being constituted as they are, i.e. not being creatures of instinct merely but possessed of intelligence and imagination which give them foresight in respect of their own affairs and make them sensitive to the presence of other people affected by the desires felt by them personally, sometimes find reasons why a particular desire felt by an individual under a certain set of circumstances should not be satisfied. And in so far as the reasons involved are justified, the pleasure at issue cannot be considered to be possessed of value.

By 'happiness' may be meant relatively permanent satisfaction and not just fleeting pleasures. When desires are looked upon merely as particular urges felt by an individual there is no guarantee that they would recur, and the pleasure derived from their satisfaction may be short-lived. Also there is no guarantee that these particular urges will not be inconsistent with one another. One's desire for a particular sort of food may be inconsistent with one's desire to enjoy health, and the one cannot then be satisfied without the frustration of the other. The fulfilment of a desire can lead to a satisfaction which is relatively permanent if a measure of consistency is achieved between the prominently felt desires of an individual. Also, if the desire, the fulfilment of which gives satisfaction, is fragmentary (i.e. unrelated to other desires), the pleasure is not only momentary, it leaves no effect beyond itself; whereas if it is related to other desires, the pleasure spreads from itself, so to say, and augments or reinforces other pleasures to be derived from related desires. To have relatively permanent satisfaction it is necessary for an individual not only to have desires that are mostly consistent but also to develop a system of desires that grows around purposes which show some sort of unity or affinity besides being in conformity with the capabilities of the individual. For unless the purposes are such that it lies within the abilities of the individual to fulfil them it is impossible for him to achieve relatively permanent satisfaction. Of course, an individual may have more than one system of desires, and these when considered together may be conceived to form what we may call 'the total life plan' of an individual. I have no wish to suggest that any such plan is consciously made by anyone or that it has a thoroughly unitary character. Some such plan may be read out of an individual's life instead of its being present in the mind of the person concerned. In any case the unity involved in such a plan is so general that it allows of differences and variations at various lower levels of classification of purposes. But it is impossible for anyone to achieve relatively permanent satisfaction without achieving a measure of integration and harmony in one's character.

By 'happiness' is also meant a deeper and richer kind of feeling and awareness than are involved in the above two senses of the term. It means an underlying feeling of joy (which is more akin to bliss than to pleasure) and gratefulness in being alive which permeates one's approach to life, on the whole. It is possible to have a lot of pleasures and relatively permanent satisfactions in life and yet lack an overall feeling of joy and gratefulness in being able to participate in the business of life, and without this one cannot be happy in any pervasive sense. This sort of happiness depends upon the satisfaction of higher self-creative needs (needs which are peculiarly human and yet not leading, by their very nature, to conflict and disharmony within one's own self and society). Yet happiness of this pervasive kind is not devoid of all elements of pleasure and satisfaction. For how can a man be grateful to be alive unless some of his instinctive needs, those which serve the purposes of an individual without being destructive of the purposes of others, are satisfied. Similarly, one cannot feel fulfilled without pursuing definite aims compatible with one's predominant nature and capabilities which only can lead to relatively permanent satisfaction. But the state which is called 'being truly happy' involves more than pleasure or satisfaction. I venture to suggest that this is dependent on achieving a sense of worth in one's own personality and this worth lies in the pursuit of intrinsic values, values which appear worthwhile pursuing for their own sakes and not for the sake of any narrowly conceived individual purpose. Without this sense of worth which goes beyond the satisfaction of private purposes an individual is likely to be harassed at times by a feeling of not being all that one could be and ought to be, provided, of course, he is sufficiently sensitive to feel the higher self-creative needs (which perhaps most human beings are, at least potentially). And this feeling detracts from much of the value of the pleasures and satisfactions that he would otherwise enjoy. (Those who cannot feel the higher self-creative needs at all, if there be any such people, remain shut out of the deeper and richer kind of happiness even though they may enjoy a great deal of pleasure.)

Happiness, then, in the most comprehensive sense of the term, means an overall feeling of joy and gratefulness on the part of an individual in being alive which permeates his existence, as well as the thought that on the whole the needs and calls that he has fulfilled or is fulfilling are the most worthy, as far as his person and capabilities are concerned, of being valued, although this does not imply that the individual concerned considers it impossible to do any better. This, of course, is the ideal limit and in actual fact one approximates this state only more or less. Also, happiness, in spite of its being most desirable for everyone, is a highly individual goal. No two individuals are made the same way and the needs and calls one feels are relative to one's temperament and capabilities which differ between different individuals. Everyone then has to work out his own manner of living which will give him, as a particular individual, the most happy existence possible. But it is necessary, if we are talking about the pervasive kind of happiness, that whatever someone may do with his life or whichever way he may adopt in his life as the best way for his purposes and person, it must be consistent with, and contributory to, intrinsic values. It is this richer kind of happiness that is the implicate of all value points of view if intrinsic values are included amongst them. (When we consider only the instrumental values all that we find implied are pleasures and satisfaction and not necessarily happiness in the comprehensive sense.)

What I have said so far distinguishes value facts from non-value facts, for non-value facts do not necessarily imply the desirability of happiness as value facts do. I have already touched on the difference between intrinsic and instrumental values. Let us now see how moral values differ from other intrinsic values.

Amongst the intrinsic values the value of morality has a certain priority because of two considerations. The realization of the values embodied in the notions 'knowledge' and 'aesthetic quality' to any considerable extent presupposes in the individual concerned certain abilities of a high degree, namely, intellectual ability and imaginative sensitivity, and such abilities may not be present in all. The value that is called 'morality' presupposes in a person a degree of intelligence and emotional sensitivity that are thought to be present in ordinary people (i.e. those who are not abnormal or sub-normal). It is thus thought that even if an ordinary man is not capable of showing regard for any other value to any considerable extent he is capable, by nature, of showing regard for morality and through this of achieving worth in his personality. The other reason for the priority of moral values is this. The pursuit of intellectual or aesthetic values is a pursuit that is not so much social as individual in character. A man's care for knowledge or aesthetic quality is induced not by consideration for other people but by his own nature which urges him towards its direction even though other people may eventually profit from his pursuit. A man's devotion to moral values is initiated through his consideration for others even though it ultimately serves him by giving worth to his personality. And as individuals can live as individuals only in a society the realization of values that are primarily individual in character is dependent in some ways on the realization of values which gives harmony to social existence. Because of this bearing of moral values on harmonious social co-existence—a state under which only individuals can realize themselves as such—it is required of every individual that he should respect them. Also, if a man's pursuit of his own purposes clashes with his harmonious existence with others, it is bound to produce in him, if he is sufficiently sensitive and capable of the richer kind of happiness, a feeling of lack of worth which will make joy hard to appear. Further, as ordinary people who are not exceptionally gifted in any way may try to achieve moral values, it is possible for them to achieve fulfilment and happiness through achieving whatever purposes suit their abilities and inclinations consistently with respect for moral values.

We thus see that moral values imply not only the desirability of happiness, as other intrinsic values also do, but also a state of affairs which we may call the greatest good, i.e. a state in which it is possible for an individual to be as happy as it is in his nature to be *in conformity with* the similar happiness of all others. I do not think that other intrinsic values imply this. This conception of greatest good, I like to emphasize, is different from that of the greatest good of the greatest number, for in this latter conception people are lumped together in a totality and the idea of individual persons, each striving to fulfil himself consistently with the requirements of morality, is somehow lost. Consistency with, and being contributory to, the conception of greatest good are then the characteristics of that value approach to experience which we call morality. The other characteristic difference of moral values lies in their reference. Moral values refer to such dispositions and principles on which such dispositions are based as are not dependent on any particular type of human ability like the intellectual or aesthetic ability and as may be formed through training and discipline even though not initially given. Further, these dispositions are characterized by implying conduct towards persons considered as ends in themselves rather than towards things.

CHAPTER VI

The Concept of Good

We shall now consider what is meant by the term 'good' in morals. The term 'good', we know, is used as a general term to express every kind of value. Because of this it is sometimes suggested, as by E. F. Carritt in his *Theory of Morals*, that it is better not to use this term in Ethics. This I do not think is possible. The concept of 'good' serves an essential purpose in our moral thinking by explaining the authority the ideas of some ends (attitudes, dispositions, states of affairs acceptable as worthwhile for their own sakes) have over our moral choice. This use of the term is one amongst the various uses that are actually made of it, but it is a distinctive use and we cannot dispense with it as long as we are to recognize the value of certain features of our experience in a moral context which are expressed by means of this concept.

Stevenson in his *Ethics and Language* attacks the idea of intrinsic ends on the ground that an emphasis on this tends to make us ignore using reasons about matters of fact and about questions of means which form the most important part of Ethics. There is no doubt a doctrine to be found in some quarters that the distinction of means and ends is such that one is justified in adopting any available means in order to achieve certain ends which are recognizable to be worthwhile. And admittedly this doctrine holds true in certain contexts. But strictly speaking this distinction is not a significant one as far as intrinsic moral ends are concerned. What are called intrinsic ends in morals are not like particular objects, like a house or a car which one may acquire by different means, or even a particular state of affairs like a peace treaty which may be achieved on honourable or dishonourable terms. The conceptions of these ends are conceptions of value-standards in accordance with which the moral worth of human personalities, character, conduct, relations, and states of affairs is judged. These are, in other words, standards for human beings for living well, which, speaking morally, is doing well. If these standards are ends which it is worthwhile for us to try and realize in our moral endeavours they are no less means for living a life that is morally worthwhile. In short, they are not the sort of ends which stand over against various alternative means, some to be recommended, others not.

Coming to the question of defining ethical terms, Stevenson says that these terms are used in different senses, and they are vague as far as usage goes. Although certain factors at any one time are definitely included among the designata of the terms and certain others excluded, there are certain others which are neither included nor excluded. The limits of the undecided region are so subject to fluctuation with varying contexts and varying purposes that it becomes arbitrary, so far as common usage is concerned, to specify where one sense of the term leaves off and another begins. But it is not easy to see what exactly Stevenson has in mind here. It is true that certain terms, particularly terms of assessment, are used in many different ways, sometimes even within the same context of discussion. It would therefore be arbitrary to say that they are not used in this way. But would it be arbitrary to say that the significance of a term used should be limited by the context in which it is used, simply because such limit is not always observed by people? I do not think that this is tenable. On the contrary, it appears to be a legitimate concern on the part of a philosopher to find out what these several meanings of a term are, as limited by the contexts in which it is used. It is surely possible to define a term by reference to a particular context in which it is applied in human speech and it is only thus that a confusion between different meanings can be avoided. The definition that Stevenson advances of the ethical term 'good', namely 'I approve of it', is an omnibus definition which is designed to cover every shade of meaning that anyone could possibly wish to express by it and this fails to tell us what the use of the term is in a distinctively ethical context. Stevenson's definition has two parts—a declarative statement 'I approve of it' which expresses the attitude of the speaker, and an imperative statement 'do so as well' which is addressed to clarifying or intensifying the attitude of the hearer. These two meanings may be implied in the various possible uses of the term 'good', but exactly how does this knowledge remove our confusion as Stevenson demands a definition should do? For surely confusion arises not because one fails to understand that the speaker approves of what he refers to as good and would like the listener to do the same as well but because one is not quite clear as to the ground on which what is being approved is approved. And it is this latter understanding that we are primarily in need of for the purposes of clarity of thought.

Stevenson argues that one can give reasons for one's attitudes of approval. Although imperatives cannot be proved, are there not reasons or arguments which may at least support them? Nevertheless the attitudes, as far as the question of defining them is concerned, remain obstinately emotive; for a definition has to cater for attitudes which are well-grounded as well as attitudes which refuse to be changed through knowledge of facts that are morally relevant. But an attitude need not necessarily be emotive. The concept of attitude is an explanatory concept whose function is to point to the relation that there is between certain characteristic ways of behaving, emotional or otherwise. (I shall presently elaborate this point.) This notion then has an emotive significance. But to say that the meaning of the term 'good' is emotive is to claim more than that. It is to say that the distinctive nature of what is morally good is that it arouses the emotion of approval. If arousing the emotion of approval is only one element amongst others and not the most characteristic one which distinguishes the ethical ideal of good from what is not good, then the notion of good does not specifically merit the name 'emotive'. It would perhaps be agreed that the emotion of approval may be aroused by what is good, as well as by what is bad or indifferent from the moral point of view. And this means that arousing the emotion of approval is not the characteristic meaning of good as far as Ethics is concerned.

The other meaning of 'this is good' is 'this has qualities or relations X, Y, Z . . .' except that 'good' has as well a laudatory emotive meaning which permits it to express the speaker's approval, and tends to evoke the approval of the hearer.

This is not a definition of 'good' but a formal schema for a whole set of definitions. What are the variables by which the schema may be replaced? It will not do, says Stevenson, to admit of any substitution whatsoever, for certain descriptive meanings will be obviously unsuitable according to our linguistic habits or usage. Now, there is a perfectly good sense, of course, in which usage may be said to determine the meaning of terms. We must mean by a term what other people mean by it as well if we wish to be understood. But to say that a term cannot be used to mean certain things because usage would not allow it is no explanation of the meaning of a term. Rather, it tends to arouse a misconception that our linguistic habits are ultimate facts in the understanding of what we mean by words. From Stevenson's account it appears that the reason why we cannot say 'stealing is good' is that it is not in our linguistic habit to do so. But no social habit is unalterably fixed and if people start referring to stealing as good we shall be justified in thinking that it is good.[1] Now, it is not to be denied that we can learn to use words only by learning or more or less unconsciously assimilating the uses other people make of them. But words are no more than symbols for recognizable aspects of our experience and when people use them in common and agree about statements in which such words are used it means that they are referring to certain aspects experienced by them in the same or a similar way. To form a language habit is not a case of mechanical manipulation or blind imitation; it is to be able to refer intelligently, whenever any need for it arises, to certain features which are experienced by the hearer in the same or corresponding ways as they are by the speaker. The nature of our experience therefore is a factor in determining the meaning of words and plausibility of usage is relative to it. If it is true

[1] Stealing from foreigners is actually considered to be good in some primitive societies. See *Experiments in Living*, Macbeath.

I

that usage determines the variables by which we can replace X, Y, Z in Stevenson's schema of definition of good, it is no less true that usage itself grows through reference to more or less stable features of experience that can be had in common between different people. There is thus a deeper reason why we cannot replace X, Y, Z by any variable we like than the fact that the way words are used is more or less settled. It is that the way we use words is limited by the nature of experience that we have in common with other people. If we use a word to refer to an aspect of experience in respect of which it is not used by other people and for which there already exists a different word, then it either ignores or opposes other people's experience and thereby ceases to be a symbol significant for purposes of thought and communication in respect of a common world.

Stevenson concludes that the word 'good' is strongly emotive and vague, and this is true of all other ethical words. A purely intellectual analysis of ethical terms like Sidgwick's definition of a just man as one who does not let himself be unduly influenced by personal preferences has, according to him, veiled and confused emotive meaning. To say that a just man does not let his personal preferences unduly influence him is to say that he does not let his personal preferences influence him more than he ought to and to use the word 'ought' is, in Stevenson's opinion, to express an emotive attitude. If this is the case then Sidgwick is defining a just man as one who does not let his personal preferences influence him in a way which he (Sidgwick) disapproves of. If Sidgwick says in reply that he disapproves of the way in question because it is unjust, and not that he thinks it is unjust because he disapproves of it, then Stevenson has little justification in insisting that Sidgwick has confused his emotive attitude with an objective state of affairs that can intellectually be analysed. It is surely not impossible for us to understand what Sidgwick means when he is talking about a person not being influenced by personal preferences, without our having any knowledge of his emotional states. It might be said in reply that we cannot but know of his emotional states when we hear him say 'a just man, etc.'. But exactly what do we know? We know that he has an emotion of approval. But do we know any more about this *emotion itself as a state of feeling* so that by understanding its distinctive characteristics we understand the ethical significance of Sidgwick's statement? And we have to have this knowledge if the significance or meaning of Sidgwick's statement has to be understood in terms of his emotion considered purely as a state of the speaker. For suppose someone says 'It is very good that you managed to escape the Customs'. We know that the speaker is expressing an emotion of approval, but we also know that the sort of attitude expressed here is not the same as Sidgwick is expressing. But we cannot explain how they differ if we keep merely to feelings. If we wish to understand their difference we shall have to understand the difference between objects which give rise to the emotions of approval that people feel, and the difference between contexts to which they are suitable. It might, of course, be said that in so far as these attitudes express an emotion of approval they are identical. But this ignores a recognizable distinction that there is between these two attitudes and insofar as we recognize this distinction it is true to say that the meaning of terms that express attitudes cannot be understood merely by reference to an emotional state. Thus we would not understand the meaning or the ethical significance of Sidgwick's statement even if we understood that he is expressing an emotion of approval when he is saying 'a just man, etc.'.

Moore argues in his *Principia Ethica* that ethical statements are more than statements of personal approval or disapproval; for when we say that something is morally good our purpose is to refer to some quality of that which is good, and this may be understood in common by the speaker and the spoken to. What then is this quality? Moore says that it is impossible for us to define the term 'good', just as it is impossible for us to define the term 'yellow', both of which stand for a quality simple and unanalysable. We cannot define 'yellow', none the less we know the quality that is meant by it. Similarly, our inability to define 'good' does not stand in the way of our understanding what is meant when someone says 'personal affection is good'. Good is a unique quality which cannot be expressed in terms of anything but itself and if we attempt to define it by saying 'good is pleasure', 'good is evolved', or some such thing, we commit the naturalistic fallacy. To say 'pleasure is good' is different from saying 'good is pleasure'. The former is a synthetic proposition, the latter is analytic, i.e. here good and pleasure stand for one and the same thing and this clearly is false. A definition of good can only be an analytic proposition and in such a proposition the unique quality of good is lost.

Moore's criticism of Naturalism has indeed been of great service to Ethics as he believed it would be, for it brings home to us afresh the important fact that the distinctive nature of morality cannot be realized merely in terms of non-value facts. But his theory that the quality 'good' is simple and absolutely unanalysable cannot be said to have positively helped our understanding of moral values. As has been pointed out by various thinkers, if good is as simple as yellow, why is there not the same conformity of opinion as to what, amongst the existing states of affairs, we may call good as there is about what objects are yellow in colour? If good is a complex notion then there can be nothing against its being analysable, although it may not be analysable into what is not of moral value. Perhaps this is what he had in mind when he called it unanalysable. How then shall we define the characteristically ethical use of the term 'good'?

The most consistent use of the term from the point of view of morality is in respect of certain human motives, attitudes (relatively permanent tendencies in an individual's reaction to situations of a certain sort), dispositions (settled habits of behaving in characteristic ways), and character (which stands for the characteristic connection that there is between an individual's actions, motives, attitudes and dispositions) as well as states of affairs that are consistent with the existence of motives, attitudes, dispositions and character that are morally good. To say this is not to deny that the term 'good' is actually used in many other ways in a moral context. But it seems to me that if there is to be a use of the term 'good' which is specifically moral we must try to discern a characteristic and consistent use of it from amongst the various actual uses that are made of it. To say that a term has a characteristic use is to say that the objects referred to by it have some discernible features by virtue of which they may be consistently thought of as similar to one another or as forming a relatively specifiable and distinguishable context of discourse. We may then define the conception of moral good as the conception of motives, attitudes, dispositions, character and states of affairs involving human relations which are consistent with the conception of greatest good and which may, generally speaking, be considered to be attainable through human effort, insofar as they do not necessarily exist without such effort, and insofar as they can exist without necessarily implying the exercise of any inherited ability of a high degree, like more than average intelligence, aesthetic imagination and susceptibility, or abundance of vital energy and so on. This is not a simple way of defining 'good' but the complexity of the whole conception makes it impossible to define it simply. No doubt the definition attempted here can be improved upon, and I have no wish to claim finality. All that I am concerned with in this definition is to emphasize the characteristic features of all that can consistently be referred to as good from the moral point of view. This definition is, as Moore says all definitions are, analytic, and it is true to say that it reveals nothing new to people who are familiar with moral conceptions. This is how it should be, for I am not here dictating terms to all who wish to understand morality but merely trying to formulate in a systematic way certain implications of the point of view of morality.

I shall now try to analyse somewhat in detail how the attitudes and dispositions that are usually considered to be morally good are characterized in the way I have spoken of in the definition of good attempted above. But perhaps it is necessary, to avoid certain misunderstandings, to explain how I am using the term 'attitude'. To say that one has an attitude, says Ryle, is to say that one is likely to behave in such and such ways in such and such circumstances. That Mr X has a patriotic attitude means that Mr X can be expected to behave (i.e. think, feel and act) in certain ways in situations of a certain sort involving his country.

For instance, he is likely to feel happy when he finds that his country is winning in what he considers to be a just war, to have concern and worried thoughts when he finds that his country is losing, to be ready and eager to do things he is able to do for his country when a need for it arises and so on. But it seems to me that we mean more than that, we mean that some of the ways in which Mr X is likely to think, feel or act when his country is concerned are characterized by being connected and consistent with one another in a way in which other ways of thinking, feeling and acting are not consistent with them. For instance, if we find that a man is expressing great concern over the future of his country and yet is not willing to do something he is able to do for improving its condition, we shall not believe that he is patriotic (we shall say 'he is not *really* patriotic'); or, if we know of a man that he is fond of going to the pictures and thinks that boxing should be made illegal we shall not conclude that he is patriotic. The conception of an attitude has an explanatory function over and above that of describing possible or actual occurrences. It serves as an explanation of the fact that some of the tendencies that an individual has to think, feel and act in certain ways are characterized by being connected and consistent with one another in that particular manner which we find to be the case.

Let us now discuss the attitudes and dispositions that are morally good. The conceptions of these attitudes and dispositions belong to different levels of abstraction and generality in our thinking about human conduct. We say something relatively concrete and more directly informative about a man when we say 'he is honest' than when we say 'he is a great man'. The most abstract and general of all the conceptions of attitudes or dispositions that are morally good is the conception of greatness which is expressed through the conceptions of attitudes or dispositions relatively less general and abstract like wisdom. One of the ways in which wisdom is manifested in moral life is through an attitude which we may call 'regard for moral value or virtue'. Moral virtues may be conceived to be of two different kinds, self-regarding and other-regarding. There is, of course, no hard-and-fast distinction between the two, for man is a social being and almost all his actions and attitudes affect others. Yet it is useful to make this distinction for certain purposes. Honesty, for example, we shall say is a self-regarding virtue, for it is possible that a particular dishonest act would not bring about any noticeable harm to a person against whom it is committed; but it harms the character of the person who commits it from the point of view of the ideal of perfection in character.[1] Amongst the most abstract and general of self-regarding moral virtues is one's desire for self-knowledge with a view to attaining worth in one's character and personality. The understanding of the value of self-knowledge is shown in such relatively specific attitudes as trustworthiness, steadfastness, courage, patience, perseverance, etc. Trustworthiness is again manifested through still more specific attitudes like sincerity, honesty, etc. Amongst other-regarding virtues the most abstract and general is what we may, for want of a better word, express by 'social consciousness', which is shown in such attitudes or dispositions as benevolence and righteousness. Benevolence is shown in such relatively specific attitudes as kindness, charity, sympathy, friendliness, etc., and the disposition of righteousness shows itself in the desire to do one's duty in general and in respecting justice in particular. This is a rough classification only, but some such classification is necessary in order to show what function these ideas play in our moral thinking about human character.

The idea of greatness is the idea of a disposition to respect some value to such a degree as not to be willing to compromise with it on account of personal pleasure, comfort, security and sometimes even life itself. It expresses our notion of the intrinsic value of a disposition to the highest possible degree that is humanly conceivable. And the function of this notion is to explain some of the conduct of exceptional individuals who place what is or are of value for human beings above everything else as evidenced in their behaviour pattern in general. When we say somebody or other is a great man we do not mean that he has realized or is realizing all the values that are humanly achievable. We only

[1] Honesty is self-regarding when it is thought of as a character trait as when a man takes just pride in being honest. But considered as activities it is other-regarding as well.

refer to his actual respect for value in some particular sphere or in particular spheres. This ideal is, of course, only more or less achievable. And the requirements of this ideal—covering as it does almost all the behaviour of an individual in a certain context or in certain contexts—are too high to be achievable in any considerable degree by people in general. That does not mean that this idea is a pure fiction, for it is in the light of this conception that we understand and appreciate the character of those who give evidence of fearlessness and dignity in upholding something that is of primary importance from a value point of view. This idea is consistent with the conception of greatest good. And although only a few exceptional people are able to achieve this to any degree, we may still include this notion amongst what are morally good, as it is possible for all of us—unless we are incapacitated for special physiological or psychological reasons—at least to try to realize it as far as we can (within the limitations of our nature) in our day-to-day moral behaviour.

One of the ways in which greatness of character expresses itself is wisdom. The notion of wisdom is the notion of a disposition which seeks comprehensiveness in the practical approach to an issue and it is based on the habit of attending carefully to everything that is relevant to the matter under consideration from the point of view of achieving as much value, both intrinsic and instrumental, as is possible under a specific set of circumstances. Real circumstances of life are complex and there are often many sides to an issue which involves questions of value. A man is said to be wise when he recognizes and understands the comparative importance of all that are concerned in a complex situation and gives them their due weight in arriving at decisions. He is careful not to be biased in favour of factors in some way convenient to himself, nor is he likely to ignore them completely unless this is specifically called for. He understands that what is desirable may not necessarily be what is desired, but he strives to desire that which is desirable, as it is only thus that a feeling of worth may be had in life. In short, the conception of a wise man is the conception of a person who is disposed towards attaining that delicate balance which is based on the understanding of the comparative importance of all that is involved in one's approach to experience that raises questions of value.

Now, to possess wisdom is not like possessing a particular skill, like, say, playing the violin, which is shown in specific types of situations and actions. It is to have a characteristic kind of approach to many different kinds of situations. To understand that a man is wise is to understand how his reactions are appropriate on the whole and in the long run to situations in which we ask how far that which has been achieved is worthwhile. Like greatness, wisdom is the conception of a disposition which is possessed by people more or less. Also one may be wise in some ways and not in others.

Wisdom is manifested through dispositions and attitudes of a comparatively less general kind, amongst which is regard for moral values or virtues. This should be referred to as a disposition if it were to mean that an individual never compromises where moral values are concerned. That will be a perfectly virtuous disposition. But an attitude of regard for moral values may exist even though the moral agent is not virtuous in every possible way. The presence of this attitude means that the agent has a positive resistance against doing anything that is objectionable from the point of view of morality. How far he is successful in withstanding the pressure of temptation depends upon the nature and intensity of his felt needs that conflict with the realization of values, upon the strength of the specific habits that he must have if he is to act satisfactorily from the point of view of morality and upon the degree of integrity of his character which helps one not to be moved too easily in situations which are novel and when the type of action one is required to perform is not covered by established habits. To have regard for moral values is to have a tendency to behave in certain ways which are consistent with one another—for example, to follow established rules and recognized principles when there is no satisfactory reason for not doing so, to give careful consideration to conflicting principles which may be relevant to a situation and to follow the one whose demand is most urgent as far as one can make it out, to exercise pressure on one's own desires which conflict with the performance of duties, to feel compunction and remorse at one's own neglect of duty, to approve behaviour like this in other human beings and to disapprove the contrary and so on. It is possible for people to have it in some ways and not in others. This regard is consistent with the conception of greatest good and its cultivation does not require the exercise of any special skill or ability.

This conception helps us to explain the presence of dispositions and attitudes which are of a more specific kind amongst which is an attitude which is sometimes referred to as self-knowledge. This is an attitude which orients one to gain knowledge of one's own self with a view to achieving moral perfection or a sense of worth and fulfilment. This is an important moral attitude. Many moral situations are such that the actions to be performed stand over against the immediate interest of the agent. It is therefore important for him to understand, from the point of view of what is possessed of value for its own sake, how to choose between the various interests that press upon him. Self-knowledge, as is the case with wisdom, is not a body of specific information about one's own nature as understood purely psychologically. Rather, it stands for a characteristic attitude towards one's own impulses, inclinations, desires and needs as they are actually felt. One shows this attitude when one asks questions as regards the most prominent needs of one's own nature, whether they can legitimately claim satisfaction (i.e. whether they are in conformity with the demands that can be made on the agent by other people), whether certain of the desires felt are consistent with the most predominant needs of the person through the satisfaction of which the agent can achieve a sense of fulfilment, and whether they are consistent with and conducive to achieving worth. One also shows this attitude when one asks about one's own abilities as well as limitations and shortcomings and accepts them when these are brought to one's notice; and it is thus that one faces life with a degree of security and self-confidence which is reasonable for one to possess. Self-knowledge thus includes the attitudes of self-criticism, self-control and what is sometimes called calmness or tranquillity. Also these attitudes, of course, may be present in different degrees or shown in different directions.

The character traits through which one shows knowledge of one's own self[1] that are morally relevant are straightforwardness, trustworthiness, courage, patience, perseverance, etc.; we call a man trustworthy when we find that he is habituated to respect the confidence which people place in him, either implicitly or explicitly, except in cases where there are justifications for not doing so. Our conduct which involves other people's trust is of different kinds and such conduct may concern our speech, our emotions and our actions. For instance, we may talk about a certain thing X in a certain fashion which we know would naturally lead someone to believe that we hold opinion Y about it. Now, we shall be violating his trust in us which he may have no reason for not having if we really hold opinion Z while he acts on the supposition that we hold opinion Y; or again if we behave in a way which would give him the impression that we are going to perform action P, thus producing a natural expectation for it while actually performing Q, we are also violating the trust which people normally place in us. Such behaviour is explained in terms of an attitude which is usually called insincerity and its opposite is called sincerity which characterizes our conduct in different degrees. Also, we may be sincere in some respects and insincere in others. Similarly, a man is said to be honest if in his dealings with people he neither takes any more from them than it is reasonable to expect is his due, nor gives them any less than it is reasonable to expect is their due. One can be honest not only in financial transactions but in any situation of social intercourse. As is the case with any other attitude, we may be honest in different degrees and in different ways.

Courage which is shown in the willingness to sacrifice personal needs (which sometimes includes even the need to be alive) in the service of some end, as well as in the willingness to endure

---

[1] It is likely that the word 'self' here would be objected to as symbolic of some metaphysical entity. But here it is used only in the sense of a conception which explains the characteristic connection that there is between all the impulses, desires, needs, feelings, emotions, thoughts and actions that can usually be attributed to one centre of experience (i.e. a person). And we cannot deny that the thoughts and purposes of one person, however multifarious and varying they may be, have a certain connection and continuity with one another which they do not have with the thoughts and purposes of another person.

pain and suffering, is another attitude through which one shows one's understanding of one's own self from the point of view of morality. It is hardly conceivable, human nature being what it is, that anyone can live a worthwhile life (i.e. life which may be judged to be relatively satisfactory on the strength of some standards of intrinsic worth) without meeting with oppositions which are sometimes of great magnitude. It is in dealing with these oppositions that one shows the attitude (if it is expressed in particular fields only) or disposition (expressed in all or most fields) which we call courage. It may here be said that circumstances of human existence may be made so favourable for all that the necessity for enduring pain and suffering or the necessity for readiness to take personal risks will no longer be felt. No doubt some of the sufferings which one needs to undergo and some of the risks one has to take in a society of a particular nature may be removed by altering some of the relations and arrangements of the society in question. But there are certain unfavourable circumstances which are beyond human control (as far as we can tell)—death of one's own near ones, for example, or physical deficiency, or inability to achieve what one wants to achieve due to short-comings of one's own nature—and one would still need courage in coping with these. Moreover, it cannot be considered desirable, human beings being what they are, that a man's environment should be made so favourable that there is never any opposition between him and his environment. For man's happiness consists in the pursuit of excellence of some form or other and this pursuit gains in strength and scope through the overcoming of oppositions met in the way. Human potentialities do not necessarily develop as a process of natural growth and quite often they need to be drawn out. One of the ways in which this is done is by setting onself a task somewhat above one's immediate reach, so that one has to persist in trying to do one's best in the face of oppositions that temporary frustrations cause. There is no one specific way in which one could show courage, also one could be courageous in some respects and not others.

Coming to discuss the virtues which are sometimes called other-regarding, the most general attitude through which regard for moral virtues is shown is interest in other people and in social affairs generally. Human beings necessarily live in a society. What an individual person becomes and the values that he realizes depend to a great extent on the contribution of other members of the society[1] in maintaining and further improving its institutions, laws, etc. It is, therefore, only becoming that an individual who appreciates the value of the characteristic kind of existence that is human should have interest in other individuals who play a part in shaping social affairs and in social affairs themselves. I am not implying that there are people who are entirely devoid of all social consciousness. But there can be more or less of it, and it is the people who have the lowest degree of it who are usually referred to as lacking in social consciousness.

Social consciousness is manifested through attitudes and dispositions which are relatively more specific, like those of benevolence and righteousness.

We call a man benevolent when he shows a tendency to think sympathetically about the distresses, sufferings and wants of people in society who are in some ways in need of help (whether or not they can be said to deserve it in any strict sense), to feel it sufficiently strongly as to be moved towards action, and to act, as far as that is within one's power, with a view to alleviating the causes which make such suffering necessary. To be benevolent is to be ready to do much more than what others can, strictly speaking, expect of one. It no doubt implies that one is in a position to render specific help, the need for which exists to any noticeable extent. One may be in this position because one has, say, financial resources, or leisure to devote to others' purposes, or because one is possessed of a special skill or ability, like knowledge of medicine which may be usefully employed to deal with some human problems.

This attitude of benevolence is quite compatible with the satisfaction of one's own felt needs unless such needs are to be considered unjustified for some reason or other, but it is equally

---

[1] The term 'society' here, of course, does not denote an entity but stands for a conception that explains the characteristic connection that there is between the different institutions, practices, traditions, customs, laws etc., which bind a group of people together by distinguishing them from every other such group.

compatible with their sacrifice if this is specifically called for and the agent is disposed to do so. But the duty of benevolence is not the duty, as such, of sacrificing one's own desires and needs. It is the duty of employing the fund of energy, ability or resources, which people may have to a greater degree than is expected to be exhausted in the pursuit of their personal ends, for the purposes of others. To be benevolent is not to do anything in particular but to be ready to do a variety of things as and when a situation demands. It shows itself through attitudes and dispositions of a more specific kind like kindness, charity, sympathy, friendliness, etc. These are allied tendencies. Kindness, for example, is shown in one's willingness to confer benefits (of different kinds) on others, charity in rendering financial assistance and help, sympathy in the imaginative sensitiveness to others' pleasures and pains, and friendliness in considerateness and agreeableness of conduct.

Some moralists have considered love to be a moral virtue. There is no doubt that the emotion of love which stands for the affection of one person for another for his own sake is one of the intrinsic values to be cherished by human beings. But if by love we mean the kinds of emotion that exist between parents and children, brothers and sisters, and between man and woman, it does not appear, according to the definition of good here adopted, to be a moral good. Love, understood as an emotional relationship, is necessarily selective and between husband and wife conceived to be exclusive (at least in some kinds of marriage). The spontaneity of affection that exists between parents and children and brothers and sisters is conditioned by instinctive urges and by close sharing of somewhat the same experiences. The marriage relation is entered into with an explicit or implicit undertaking to maintain the exclusiveness of the relation, and the central importance of one party for another is here understood and voluntarily accepted. The bond of affection here grows spontaneously through the interplay of some deeply felt urges of human nature, physical and mental. The love that is required of an individual for his fellow beings cannot predominantly be a state of affection (in the sense of an emotional overflow), for this is spontaneous and not so much the result of effort. Cultivating universal love is really a matter of cultivating kind thoughts and considerate feelings as far as that is possible. In short, it is a matter of developing sympathy, kindness and friendliness towards those for whom one feels no spontaneous affection.

The characteristic kind of relationship which we call 'friendship' and which is considered to be a moral value, of course, implies much more than the attitude of friendliness that can be universally cultivated. For friendship is also to a great extent exclusive, and it involves the emotional state of affection. But it differs from other love relationships in two important ways. A relation of friendship grows out of free choice as opposed to a blood relation which is given. It has not got a contractual character that is socially enforceable as has the marriage relationship. The mutual repect, kind consideration and affection which friends have for each other are thus given and received throughout the course of friendship out of free choice of the individuals concerned. (We are here concerned only with that particular type of friendship which grows out of kindred dispositions and is not cultivated for any other purpose than friendship itself, or with friendship in so far as it is based on a desire for friendship for its own sake.) Friendship demands more effort to maintain itself than does other love relations, as it is fed to a lesser degree by instinctive urges. But this effort, theoretically speaking, is made more freely than in other cases, as social pressure in the form of 'natural' expectations is here less evident. It is in all these that the moral relevance of friendship lies.

The usefulness of the term 'conscientiousness' lies in explaining that aspect of character which is manifested in the desire to do whatever is one's duty—the conception of duty being here a stringent one. The duty of doing some good to others is no doubt a duty but it is not considered as stringent a duty as the duty of not positively harming anyone. Of course, the distinction between what one must consider one's duty and what one may, is not always a purely ethical distinction. According to one interpretation of stringency what we must consider our duty are those which—the society we live in being of a certain kind—it is reasonable on the part of others to expect of us. We are blamed for not performing the duties that are stringent even though their performances are not particularly praised, whereas the non-performances of the less stringent duties do not call for blame, but their performances meet with special admiration. In so far as this distinction is purely ethical it appears to lie in this. Our actions may violate the value that an individual has from the point of view of morality or recognize it in different degrees. Also, the actions that an agent is obliged to perform may call for a greater or lesser degree of personal sacrifice. Those actions the non-performance of which involves the violation of the moral value of individuals to a relatively great degree as well as those the performance of which does not call for great personal sacrifice are usually called the more stringent duties.

The desire to do one's duty is a desire like any other desire. Yet it has this characteristic difference from other desires that it does not arise out of any spontaneous and natural urge but exists necessarily as a result of training and regulation of one's naturally felt urges with reference to an ideal. Conscientiousness does not require of us, as is sometimes thought, that we must always sacrifice our self-regarding desires whenever they clash in any way with those of others with whom we stand in some way related. It requires that we should not assume that our needs and purposes are any more important than the needs and purposes of other people, but not that we ourselves have no claim to consideration. To have regard for humanity we must have regard for ourselves as well. And as some of our needs and purposes are legitimate we are not morally bound to sacrifice them. To have regard for one's own self is different from being selfish. A man is said to be selfish when he is bent upon his own satisfaction in complete disregard of others. A man is said to have regard for himself when he seeks satisfaction of his desires consistently with the integration and fulfilment of his personality without interfering with the legitimate satisfaction of others. No doubt in actual life the balance is difficult to achieve. The concept of 'legitimacy' being an unspecified concept, it is hard and sometimes even impossible to tell whether in any crucial instance one is being merely self-regarding or selfish. But it is still possible for us to understand the distinction between the two types of conduct and in complex circumstances do our best by being critical of our own motives and purposes. We can ask ourselves, when we cause any frustration of others' satisfactions, whether it is reasonable on their part to expect that they should not be frustrated. That is to say, we may try to find out what reasons we have for behaving in the way we did and if these reasons will recommend themselves to morally reflective people (i.e. people who will judge the moral value of a behaviour by considering whether it is consistent with the conception that every human being, including the agent himself, is an end in himself). In view of the generality of the moral criterion it is quite possible that we shall not be able to arrive at any definite conclusion in highly complex situations and there the criterion of decision can no longer be purely conscientiousness (i.e. the stricter conception of duty). In case of instances where there is something to be said both for self-sacrifice and self-satisfaction we generally admire those who show a greater sensitiveness to other people's satisfaction than their own, however legitimate their own satisfaction may appear, although we do not blame those who do not do so. This is because a person who can take pleasure in the satisfaction of other people's needs even when it involves sacrifice of his own has altogether a more valuable personality than one who cannot do so. That is to say, he has greater potentialities for happiness than others—through the satisfaction of his own needs as well as through that of others.

Conscientiousness shows itself in dispositions and attitudes of a more specific kind amongst which are the disposition called just and the attitude of impartiality or fairness. The conception of a just disposition is the conception of a person who treats human beings as unequal only on the basis of inequalities of acquired merits and of inherited abilities of which they have given evidence. He is not happy about existing inequalities between people which may be traced merely to favourable circumstances 'given' to an individual rather than acquired by him through individual effort and ability. He prefers to see that

K

the states of affairs which affect human beings socially are not unfavourable to any group of individuals, as judged under a specific set of circumstances, from the point of view of achieving as much happiness as they are potentially able to. Now, it is by no means easy to achieve this in any aspect of social affairs which concerns multitudes of human beings differing in their abilities and needs, or even, as far as I can see, possible to achieve it to the complete satisfaction of all at any one stage. For possibilities for human fulfilment are unlimited and we can have little knowledge of an individual's inherent abilities as bereft of all environmental influences which make it possible for an ability to grow and develop. Nevertheless the idea of a just disposition has a legitimate function, that of explaining the behaviour of people who look at social organizations in general from the point of view of judging whether they are unfavourable to some members of the society in some respects for the perpetuation of which, under the circumstances as existing, there is no adequate justification.

When we say that the attitude of a man is fair or impartial in such and such respects, we usually mean that he is inclined to give due consideration (weigh the respective merits of individual needs, abilities and circumstances) to the claims of all involved in such respects, that he is careful to ensure, as far as that is possible, that his treatment of others in such respects is not influenced by personal preferences and prejudices, that he looks upon contrary treatment on the part of others as morally blameworthy, that he is willing to act, if that be within his power and province, to secure that individuals hitherto treated prejudicially in these respects are given proper considerations and so on.

A just attitude or disposition implies the desirability of a characteristic state of affairs involving human relations known by the term 'justice'. The term 'justice' is open to various interpretations. Here I shall try to expound that characteristic use of it which is consistent with the definition of moral good here adopted.

The function of the conception of 'justice' is to explain a characteristic way in which we look at some human relations and human states of affairs. The way in question requires that (1)

the relations between individual human beings should be characterized by the fact that due respect is being paid by each to the
legitimate needs and purposes of others and that (2) human states
of affairs should be arranged in such a way that each individual
has opportunities equally with others for fulfilling all his needs
of a legitimate nature and thereby of attaining as much satisfaction as he is capable of having. (This does not mean that
opportunities must be just the same for all irrespective of individual abilities to profit from them, unless, of course, human
societies develop in such a way—which they have not done so
far—that any discrimination would no longer be necessary.) This
conception acts as a standard in terms of which we judge the
satisfactoriness or otherwise of existing relations and arrangements
whenever any cause for doubt arises. This is not to say that
existing relations and states are either just or unjust. Rather
they may be considered to be just in some ways and unjust in
others or they may satisfy its requirements in different degrees.
The term 'justice' does not stand for any concrete state whose
features are of a particular nature with which existing relations
and affairs may correspond point to point or they may not do so.
It is an abstract conception which explains why we are happy
about accepting certain existing relations and affairs while
questioning others from a moral point of view. This further
explains the struggle that goes on in any particular society with
a view to changing existing relations and states to something
better from the point of view of opportunities for individual
happiness. (This is not to say that every struggle for change is a
struggle for justice.)

Justice is concerned with human needs—with the requirement
that any group or groups of individuals are not to be treated in
such a way as to assume that the needs of some have a prior claim
to fulfilment. Now, the concept of 'need' is not a purely descriptive concept; it has an explanatory function as well. That is to say,
we do not mean by the term 'need' any specific and particular
impulse or desire nor any group of such desires although what we
mean by it includes particular desires. Human desires are of
various kinds and of various degrees of intensity. They are much

more complex than impulses and are conditioned by social environment in a way what we may call a pure impulse is not. We feel an impulse to eat when we are hungry, but we usually talk of a desire to eat when we want to eat, not just anything, but something in particular, say chicken—roasted or curried according as our taste has been influenced by socially established ways of cooking. The nature of our desires, then, has a social aspect and their fulfilment is also consequent on certain established ways in the society in question. Thus the word 'need' in one of its uses, i.e. the use that is morally relevant, means— at the present stage of human history, at any rate—particular desires of individuals relative to a particular society and not something which is uniformly present in all human beings. For all human beings do not live under social conditions the existence of which is necessary before certain desires are felt and can be satisfied. When we say that a need is legitimate we mean that it can rightfully claim satisfaction in the society of a certain kind, for it can be fulfilled in conformity with the fulfilment of similar needs in other individuals and the special needs of those who have special abilities or are in special circumstances.

This is a highly general conception and it is doubtful if anything very conclusive regarding the legitimacy of quite a lot of human desires can be said on the strength of this conception. Yet some such conception is involved in some of the campaigns of social reformers for a rearrangement of particular states of affairs in a particular society so that the needs of some people—which they believe to be legitimate considering the potentialities of the society in question in respect of their fulfilment—are no longer frustrated.

Here no doubt is involved a difficulty. Societies are at different stages of development, but there is no reason to believe either that societies which are at a certain time at a low level of development in comparison with others cannot progress any further, or that societies which are comparatively highly developed cannot develop any more. This makes it difficult to apply the conception of 'need' with any degree of rigidity. Nevertheless it is at least possible, theoretically speaking at any rate, to distinguish between the actually felt desires which could be fulfilled under existing conditions if existing conditions are somewhat rearranged, and desires, if they are actually felt, which could be fulfilled if certain further developments not impossible to take place do take place. Justice requires that the first group of desires be fulfilled here and now, whereas as far as the second group of desires are concerned what is required is to develop the conditions first on which the satisfaction of desires in question is consequent. But the question of justice becomes relevant whenever certain actually felt desires are being frustrated in any particular society thereby hampering the possibility of individual happiness to some degree or other due to causes that are socially controllable.[1]

An important point which arises in connection with applying the conception of justice to concrete cases should here be mentioned. According to the account of happiness we have adopted here it is neither necessary nor desirable that every felt desire of an individual should be satisfied. But to say that an individual needs to suppress or regulate desire X for achieving a happy personality is different from saying that X is a sort of desire which justice requires some individuals in a particular society should not have a chance of fulfilling. Regulation and control of desires with a view to some purpose ought to be a matter of individual decision as far as adults are concerned. Compulsory or forced denial cannot produce a healthy and happy personality. Even if it is morally desirable that an individual should regulate his desire X it may still be desirable from the point of view of justice that social arrangements should not make the fulfilment of desire X impossible.

To say a few more words before I close this discussion on moral good. The attitudes, dispositions and states of affairs that have been under discussion here are all abstract and general conceptions although they belong to different levels of generality and abstraction. The states of affairs that we directly experience in a society are of a particular nature. For instance, we may find that

---

[1] These concepts 'legitimacy' and 'need' help us to look at human phenomena in some characteristic way. Their usefulness lies not only in definite results which we might achieve by applying them to real life situations, but primarily in the method of approach to facts which they initiate.

the educational facilities in the society X are so meagre that eighty per cent of the population remain illiterate but we do not know as directly that it is unjust. (We can say that it is unjust by knowing further that more opportunities could be provided and by looking at these two together from a different point of view altogether.) It may be true that this is unjust, but the concept 'unjust' does not describe anything that is relatively directly experienced about the educational organizations of the society; it explains the discontent that some people, however few in number, have with its indefinite continuation as well as the attempts made by some people to alter it in such a way as to give as many people as possible, at a certain stage, a chance to be educated. The state of affairs, attitudes and dispositions that have been discussed here are thus not the ones of which we have relatively direct experience in actual life. They are of the nature of conceptions or standards in terms of which we explain the judgments that we pass from the characteristic point of view that we call moral, on the states of affairs, attitudes and dispositions of which we have relatively direct experience. This is why we do not necessarily have to say that things that we directly experience are either morally good or bad, just or unjust. They may be better or worse than other things, or more or less just. Again they may be good or just in some ways and bad or unjust in others. And we can say these things on the strength of the conceptions of some standards that are acceptable as self-evident from a rational point of view.

CHAPTER VII

The Concepts of 'Ought', 'Right' and 'Duty'

The concept of duty, says Toulmin, is inextricable from the mechanics of social life and 'we can fairly characterize Ethics as a part of the process whereby the desires and actions of the members of a community are harmonized'. It is no doubt true that ethical language is in some ways concerned with the harmonious existence of the individual members of a community. But Toulmin's language tends to suggest that moral concepts are used by us as so many tools for making social existence possible, which is saying, in effect, that morality is a handmaid of sociality. This is what I wish to contest.

The very conception of social or communal life, says Toulmin, involves the idea that the individual members of the community concerned recognize, speaking generally, of course, the virtue of performing their duties. Thus, if we understand what is involved in social or communal life we also understand the implications the concept of 'duty' bears. But it seems to me that instead of its being the case—as a superficial acquaintance with Toulmin's language might lead one to suppose—that social life is brought and kept in existence by using the notion of duty as a mechanism of adjustment, a certain amount of adjustment (however little in comparison with the moral requirement) takes place wherever there is human existence because of certain primitive (not entirely learnt) ways in which human nature responds to its conditions of life. The notion of duty is of a later growth and it has to do not only with the very possibility of social existence but also with the achieving of a characteristic kind of value in individual behaviour and in social relations. Social existence is no doubt itself a value, but the concept of 'duty' aims at more than that—it aims at a characteristic kind of social existence that is in agreement with conceptions of what are desirable in human behaviour for their own sakes. I do not wish to suggest that Toulmin would deny this, but his language might easily lead some people to believe that morality is nothing other than sociality. Incidentally, it is not the concept of 'duty' alone which is intelligible in the context of social life. There are many other concepts, the concepts of 'politics', for example, or 'economics' or 'language', which are intelligible only in a social context. Social existence is a condition of all characteristically human activities. But we do not understand their nature as distinct human activities merely by understanding their social significance. And Toulmin himself says, although with reservations, that there is something more involved in moral conceptions than social existence and harmony. For even when there is harmony in social life we may enquire whether, if some specific changes were made, the members of our community would lead fuller and happier lives. But Ethics which asks this question is an extension of Ethics proper which deals with the questions of social harmony and coexistence. This distinction between Ethics proper and Ethics extended, however, appears to be an arbitrary one. For as far back as Aristotle in the history of Western thought Ethics was considered to be concerned with the question of living a good and happy life. The distinction may be useful for certain purposes as long as it is not concluded that Ethics extended is any less fundamental and important than Ethics proper.

Coming to discuss the question of 'right', Toulmin criticizes those philosophers who believe that the meaning of 'X is right' is either 'X is an instance of a rule of action' or 'X is the alternative which is likely to produce the best results'. There can be good reasons for believing that X is right. But the meaning of 'X is right' is only that it is the thing to do, to encourage others to do and so on. No doubt we mean this when we say 'X is right'. But do we not also mean that the thing to do is characterized in some distinctive way by virtue of which we consider it *worth* our recommendation from the point of view of morality? Toulmin, of course, would prefer to say that there are good reasons why the thing is to be recommended to saying that the thing to be recommended is characterized in some distinctive way; and the reasons for recommending something are not to be confused with the recommendation of the thing itself. To interpret 'X is right' as 'X is the thing to do because of *p, q, r*' (the factual reasons why X is the thing to do) is to confuse fact with value. If this is so, what Toulmin and others have called a good reason in favour of X does not quite convey what is expressed by saying 'the characteristics by virtue of which that which is said to be right is valued from the point of view of morality'. To interpret 'X is right' as 'X is characterized in such and such ways by virtue of which it is to be recommended' is not to confuse fact with value but to explicate the value of X. The apparent discrepancy between Toulmin's way of interpreting 'X is right' and the traditional way is due to the fact that by X Toulmin primarily means some particular act or some particular practice which does not recommend itself but can be supported by reasons given in its favour, whereas philosophical writers have discussed the word 'right' mainly in connection with some ways of acting in general, which are characterized in such a way as to recommend themselves to us when we look at them from a particular point of view. The fact that we can give reasons in favour of some particular action which does not obviously appear to be fitting to a situation of a specific nature need not stop us from trying to understand the distinctive nature of a type of action which does recommend itself as fitting to a type of situation (i.e. not to any specific situation in particular but to a sort of situation in so far as it is conceived to be of a certain nature that is morally relevant). I shall discuss this point presently.

The reasons that can be given in favour of a thing being right are two-fold, according to Toulmin. If it is an action which is an unambiguous instance of a maxim generally accepted in the community concerned it is right just because it is an instance of such a maxim; if it is an action over which there is a conflict of duties or which is itself a principle (or social practice) as opposed to a particular action it will be right or wrong according as its consequences are likely to be good or bad.

But suppose that the action is an instance of a practice or principle that is not recognized by the community to which the individual asking the question belongs. The immediate consequences of introducing this practice into the community may not appear, as far as one can judge such matters, to be any better than the circumstances already prevailing, in so far as a degree of unsettlement of existing arrangements and relations would be involved. Suppose that two sets of consequences, one related to the introduction of the practice X and the other to its non-existence or existence of its contrary, appear to be equally good or bad at a certain period A. Have we not any other criterion by which to judge the rightness of the practice in relation to that period? Do we not say—even though there is no appreciable difference in the measurable consequences in terms of positive hardship or suffering—practice X is better than its absence or its contrary because it shows greater justice or more respect for some people than before? This point can be illustrated by the example that Toulmin has used. Let us suppose that the practice of polygamy in a society causes a certain amount of positive hardship to some women. (Not every woman who is given in a polygamous marriage suffers consciously because of the long process of social conditioning by tradition.) Introduction of monogamy would remove such hardship but bring into being new ones, for people who are steeped in the tradition of polygamy, have grown up with certain expectations attached to this institution and have something at stake in the social and economic arrangements connected with the practice of polygamy. So long as we think merely of the suffering that can be contributed to the continuation of polygamy or its abolition there may not be very much to choose between the two at a certain stage of transition. Yet some people would say, and I believe rightly, that it would be morally better to abolish polygamy and introduce monogamy, in as much as monogamy does greater justice to women or pays greater respect to them as distinct individuals; and this holds true even in the period when monogamy is being introduced and is attended with a certain amount of suffering for some people.

It is, of course, not my intention to say that we never judge anything to be right by its consequences or that the magnitude of the consequences is not a contributory factor in actual moral evaluation. There certainly are cases where our choice between alternatives, otherwise of equal merit, is determined solely by the expected consequences, or where we choose not to adopt a principle as a guide to our action in a particular case, however commendable it may appear to be when considered on its own, if we feel that the consequence of such an action would be a great deal of suffering for a lot of people which can be avoided by avoiding the action. What I am contesting is the theory that we have said all that can be said in the matter when we have remarked that an action is right because of two reasons: (i) it is an instance of a rule of action generally accepted by the community, (ii) the consequences which follow it are good. These two reasons, amongst others, may support our particular contentions to the effect that something or other is right; but they do not exhaust all that is implied in calling something 'morally right'. And the question of the meaning of 'right' remains in spite of attempts to dissolve it as meaningless. No doubt 'X is right' does mean 'X is the thing to do' and so on, but it also means, and this is important for our purposes, that X has a distinctive nature which whatever cannot be called right has not. And it is this meaning which is philosophically most important.

I am, in this enquiry, treating the terms 'good', 'right' and 'duty' as distinct from one another in some ways. It is, of course, quite obvious that the terms 'right' and 'good' and the terms 'right' and 'duty' are often used interchangeably. But I believe these terms have also their distinct applicabilities, and in so far as this is the case it is justifiable to look for that meaning of each term which is distinguishable from that of the other two. All the three terms, of course, are moral-value terms and this explains why we can use them interchangeably for certain general purposes of moral evaluation. Now the term which is used to convey moral value in general is 'ought'. We say such things as 'he is a sort of man one ought to be' (i.e. he is a good man), or 'one ought to keep one's promises' (i.e. it is right to keep a promise), or 'you ought to visit your friend in the hospital this evening' (i.e. it is your duty to visit your friend in the hospital this evening). Perhaps a few words ought to be said about the concept of 'ought' in so far as it expresses moral value in general. It does not seem to me that there is any occasion to doubt the possibility of a genuine value experience, i.e. of a kind of experience in which one finds oneself cherishing certain things or desiring them in preference to others in that characteristic manner which fits in with the thought that the things in question are worthy of being cherished or desired not only by the agent who is actually having the experience but by others as well. A value approach to experience is then an approach which is characterized in such a way that we could say that the person valuing considers the object in question preferable to some of the objects which could be chosen or desired instead. Now, it is true that our preferences, as psychological acts, may be purely matters of taste for which no reason can either be given or asked for. But when we say that we consider an object preferable to others we say much more than that we are experiencing a feeling of preference. We imply that there is some conception of a standard—whether or not we could produce it on demand—which is acceptable by people concerned in a certain context of discourse and in terms of which the object (or objects) rejected in favour of the one chosen or desired could be considered to be less worthy of acceptance. To say that a standard is implied is not to claim that we must have a standard consciously before our minds before we start to assess things. Our actual value experiences come first; we value things or prefer them to others which could also claim our attention without perhaps any understanding of why we do so. An act of valuing, at the stage when it is unreflective and un-conscious of its implications, may be described as a characteristic kind of reaction—a reaction involving choice of certain things in preference to others—that a human personality may have to certain aspects of experience. The conception of a standard takes shape only when many such reactions have taken place—re-actions which show consistency of choice or preference of a certain kind. It takes shape through our trying to explain the persistent occurrence of a certain kind of choice in many different situations. As we formulate the idea of a standard of choice we understand the consistency in choice that we actually have come across more fully than we had done before, i.e. we understand that the consistency displayed by a certain type of choice is not accidental but is a significant occurrence. Now although it is true that one can and does value, and value in a characteristically consistent manner, without at all being conscious of applying a standard, we can say that the idea of a standard that can be formulated on reflecting on some characteristically consistent acts is logically implied in any such act. That is to say, if a man, to take a concrete example, consistently resists temptation to tell lies we would expect him to agree with our contention that the truth ought to be told. And if he does not, we shall be puzzled by his behaviour in a way in which we shall not be puzzled if he does agree.

Now the use of the word 'ought' involves the idea of obligation in some sense or other. But exactly how the idea of obligation is involved depends on whether we are talking about a particular action that ought to be done or a general state of affairs that ought to be. As far as a particular action is concerned, the obligation is personal, somebody or other in particular is obliged to do it. But when we talk about a general state of affairs we do not ascribe any obligation to anyone in particular. It is an obligation that we find belongs to human beings in general on an abstract consideration of what we believe to be essential human nature. If by 'X' we mean a general state of affairs that is to be valued, to say 'X ought to be' is to say 'X is the sort of thing that is, speaking generally, preferable in human affairs, and considered from an abstract point of view of what sort of persons human beings can be, they are, again speaking generally, under an obligation to bring it into existence.' The idea of human nature, of course, includes everything that a human being is or can be. The human nature on an abstract consideration of which a general moral obligation is imputed to human beings in general is arrived at by a process of value judgment which singles out as desirable some traits which it is not impossible for human beings to develop (except in some special cases). This abstract human nature, on which is based the idea of general obligation to bring into being that which ought to be, is then a value conception and is not a purely descriptive one in respect of what all human beings actually are as individuals.

Ross in his *Foundations of Ethics* treats the word 'ought' as more or less synonymous with 'right', when by 'right' is meant a particular action which ought to be done. Accordingly, he believes that the use of the word 'ought' always involves an idea of personal obligation. The use of the word 'ought' in 'sorrow ought to have been felt by him at his relative's death' is therefore an improper use, for it is not possible for a man to summon up sorrow then and there. One would agree with Ross that 'sorrow ought to have been felt by a man at the death of a certain relation' cannot mean that it ought to have been felt by the man, now, irrespective of the character and the actually existing sentiments of the person concerned. Or 'virtue ought to be rewarded' cannot mean that anybody in particular is obliged to reward virtue. But I do not see why the use of the word 'ought' in these sentences should be considered to be improper, i.e. why the idea of obligation involved in 'ought' should necessarily be considered as a particular or personal obligation. The use of this word certainly brings the idea of obligation to our mind, but sentences like 'one ought to tell the truth' or 'virtue ought to be rewarded' do not imply that anybody in particular at a particular time is responsible for doing anything. They only mean that, on an abstract consideration of what human nature can be, human beings in general are under an obligation to do certain things rather than others, whenever a suitable occasion arises—unless, of course, there are morally tenable reasons why they should not. A man cannot feel sorrow whenever he likes. But if sorrow is a sentiment that is fitting to the occasion of the death of a relation, human beings in general are under an obligation to cultivate it, considering that they have it in their nature to feel sorrow at certain appropriate occasions. The sentence 'sorrow ought to have been felt by X at his relative's death' might only refer to this general human obligation, or to the failure of the man in particular in discharging the obligation of cultivating a suitable human sentiment, if there is no reason to believe that the man in question is incapable of the sentiment in question. If Ross's recommendation has to be accepted, all general 'ought' sentences have to be rewritten, and instead of its functioning as a general value term in morals, as it actually does, it will have to function as a synonym for 'duty'.

Now, what actually is meant in morals by the concept of 'obligation'? To say 'X is under an obligation to do Y' is to do more than to refer to the actual doing of Y by X. The question of obligation arises not only because we want Y to be done but also because we believe certain things about the nature of X as a human being and about the nature of Y as a type of activity. That is to say, we believe that it is not only possible but in some sense natural for human beings to have inclinations which run counter to the doing of an activity of the type Y. But we also mean that in spite of its being natural in some sense that human beings would feel these inclinations it is not necessary that these must have satisfaction whenever they are felt, considering the power that human beings in general have of regulating themselves with reference to some purpose or standard. Now X being a human being we presume that it is not impossible for him to feel strong inclinations contrary to the doing of Y. But we also believe, unless there are reasons to the contrary, that he is able to control these inclinations. As regards the action in question, we believe that it represents a type of activity which is in accordance with a principle of action that appears on general considerations to be worthwhile for its own sake. To talk about the obligation of a particular person to do a particular thing, then, is to suppose that there is a general human obligation to do certain kinds of actions whenever such actions are called for. The idea of particular obligation differs from the idea of general obligation in this. To impute an obligation to do a particular act to a particular person we shall have to make sure that there are not special physiological, psychological, social or other reasons which make it impossible for the person to carry out the responsibility in question under the circumstances. The idea of general human obligation takes no account of such special factors which may be present in special circumstances and is concerned with what is possible for human beings in general on an abstract consideration of their nature.

Let us now turn to the question of the meaning of 'right' in so far as it is distinguishable from 'duty'; and when thus distinguished it refers to a principle of action rather than to any act in particular. The consequence theory advocates that an act is to be judged right if the results it brings forth are good. But some of the results of a particular act which is in some ways an instance of what is usually recognized to be a right type of activity are sometimes not good. The consequence theory has thus to fall back on the idea of 'good' usually and on the whole. Whatever be the result of telling the truth in a particular case, truth-telling usually and on the whole produces good results. One could hardly deny that this is so. But the question is, do we mean by calling something right that it produces good results? I do not believe that this position can be defended. And one of the reasons why it cannot be is this. No theory, if it is to respect practice, can advocate that no exception must ever be made to a principle. When is it right then to tell a lie? We are justified, according to the theory in question, if the consequences of doing so will be good on the whole. Now there are cases where it is possible for us to be reasonably assured that the consequences of telling a lie would be on the whole better than telling the truth. But there are also cases where we find that although the specific bad consequences that follow from telling the truth can be avoided by telling a lie, telling a lie would give rise to consequences which would be bad in other ways; and there may not be any criterion by which to assess the comparative goodness (by which rightness has to be defined) of the two sets of bad consequences.[1] How then shall we decide which would be right to do? A theorist of the consequence

[1] Suppose that it has just been found that X, although apparently healthy, is suffering from a disease which is almost incurable. The doctor who has made the diagnosis is a great friend of X and he wishes to spare X this knowledge which is bound to give him a great shock and to make life appear cheerless and without hope. Yet if after the check-up X is told that he is all right he will possibly not take any precaution and there is a chance that a failure to take certain precautions may shorten the expectation of his life. The doctor may be undecided whether it is better to live a cheerful but possibly short life or a cheerless but comparatively longer life. The ordinary opinion is, I believe, that a man should not be kept ignorant of the state of his health, particularly because if told in good time he might get used to his misfortune and decide to make the best of a bad case.

school would have to reply that in a case like this it does not matter what one does. But this would be contrary to our ordinary moral convictions. We certainly believe that in such cases as these, telling the truth would be right in spite of the bad consequences. However true it may be that the results of right acts are usually and on the whole good, we cannot understand the meaning of 'right' merely in terms of the goodness of the consequences that are somehow measurable.

Joseph says in *Some Problems in Ethics* that a right act is causally related to good. By 'good' he does not mean any one particular consequence but the whole way of life of a community. If the system or way of life of which a particular act is a manifestation is good the act is right, otherwise not. Here the words 'right act' stand for an action which is an instance of a rule manifested in an established social practice or institution. This is why the rightness of the act has to be looked for in the goodness of the way of life of the community of which the practice or institution is an integral part. But not all acts which are called right acts are instances of a social practice unless we are prepared to refer to a principle like 'one ought to tell the truth' as a social practice. But if we do so, we lose the criterion by which Joseph would determine the rightness of an act. For a principle like 'the truth ought to be told' might be accepted as a moral principle in societies (Indian and European, for example) whose ways of life may be quite different and in some ways opposed. The rightness of the principle is then independent of any particular society and cannot therefore be sought in the goodness of any way of life in particular.

There are other philosophers who find the rightness of an act in the goodness of the motive from which it springs. It certainly seems to me true to say that many of the acts that we call right do spring from motives that are good. But the question is, do we call them right because of those motives or is it that the rightness of an act has to be understood independently of any motive that may be involved? To take a concrete example. A man risks physical injury for himself in order to save a child from being run over by a car. The important motive in this

L

particular case, let us suppose, was to impress his girl friend who, he knows, suspects him of cowardice and is consequently hesitating to accept his proposal of marriage. Was this act of saving the child's life right or was it wrong on the ground that the primary motive involved was morally neutral? I do not think that anyone would say that the act was wrong, even morally wrong, because of the absence of a morally good motive. When therefore people say that this act was not right, they do not mean that what the man did was in any way unsuitable to the situation or that it was in any way improper on the part of the man to do it. They only mean that the motive of the man was not good, or not good enough; and this is not a judgment about the actual act itself. An act is right if it is fitting to a situation as viewed morally, or if it is morally called for in a situation; and it is not necessary in order that an act may be fitting to a situation that it must be the outcome of any particular motive. Morality, of course, requires both from us, that we shall do the right acts and that we shall have the good motives. But this is a different question from what is right. What is true about motive is that it is only when we have certain good motives that it can generally be expected of us that we shall act rightly. Otherwise our acting rightly is a matter of chance or accident. But this would not show that our acting rightly and our having good motives are the same or even that they are absolutely inseparable. If they were, it would not have been possible for us to say anything like 'although his motive was good what he did was not right'.

I therefore agree with Ross when he says that the question of rightness has to be understood as distinct from the question of goodness. Right acts are right for being what they are; that is to say, for being fitting to certain situations which call for actions of certain types. It is only motives, attitudes, dispositions, and character that are called good. But it is not to be concluded from this that right acts, as divorced from good motives, have no moral value. Both 'right' and 'good' are moral-value terms, only they (in so far as these two terms are distinguishable) refer to the value of different kinds of issues in a moral context. The act of saving a child's life is possessed of moral value because of the saving of the child's life that is involved (or to put it differently, because of the saving of the child's life being suitable to the situation in which his life is in danger) whatever be the motive behind it. What we can say of the situation in which a child's life is saved but in which the motive to save his life is not present is that it is lacking in some value which could also have been present in the situation along with the value of the right act, and this is the value which a good motive has as a manifestation of a good character. This rightness of the act can easily be seen if we contrast it with the absence of the act in the same situation, i.e. with the non-saving of the child's life. Kant, amongst others, fails at times to make this distinction between the moral value of a good disposition and that of a suitable act to a particular situation or that of a type of activity to situations conceived to be of a certain kind. When he says that an act is right only if it is done out of respect for the moral law he is failing to make a distinction which it is necessary to make between the two aspects of a total situation, namely the character of the agent who acts in some particular way rather than another, and the suitability of the act itself to some features of the situation which are morally relevant. It is quite possible for someone to have little respect for morality and yet do what is suitable to a situation by accident or design. However lacking in goodness the man's character may be, it does not seem possible to say that what he did was anything but right; and right in the sense of being possessed of value in so far as it is what is demanded by the situation as viewed morally.

Now the instance of saving a child's life that we have selected is simple and it would perhaps not be disputed by anyone that this action of saving the child's life was right. But it is possible to think of a situation where the question whether a child's life should be saved may cause disagreement. Suppose that the child to be saved by an intricate operation would be condemned to a life of extreme pain and suffering with very little or no possibility of pleasure and consequently of happiness (happiness is not pleasure but it cannot exist without there being the possibility of pleasure). In a case like this quite a few people might think that it would be better not to save the child's life. It would then be questioned whether the act of saving a child's life in our first instance is right because of the saving of the child's life or because of some other thing that we consider to be of value, as it is possible for an act of saving a child's life to be considered other than right. And this question is related to the question of defining 'right'.

We no doubt use the term 'right' in connection with a particular action, as when we say it was right for the man to have saved the child's life. But if we do so, we are also prepared to say that any act of saving a child's life in the same or similar circumstance (i.e. from being run over by a car) is right. There is something unreasonable about refusing to admit this general implication while accepting the particular statement. This general implication of right or legislation in respect of a type of activity rather than an action in particular—like 'it is right to save a child from being run over by a car'—is what we mean by a principle. By 'right' then as distinguishable from 'duty' (which deals with particular actions) is signified a principle of action which embodies the moral suitability of a type of action to a kind of situation or rather to a certain feature present in a situation. Now if we agree that a child ought to be saved from being run over by a car we also accept by implication a more general principle—namely, life should be preserved rather than destroyed. To say this, again, is to agree implicitly with a still more general principle: 'life should be treated as possessed of value'. Now the fact that some people would not value a life which is bound to be full of pain and suffering implies that they believe that the value of life is related to the possibility of happiness that it brings.

To pursue further the problem we have been discussing. When people do not question a particular act of saving a child from being run over they take the action to imply the suitability of a type of action embodied in a principle which shows itself to be valid, namely 'it is right to save a child from being run over'. This principle is implicitly recognized and assented to whenever a particular action of saving a child's life is acclaimed as right. But there are actions, in some ways resembling actions that will not be questioned by anyone, which some may question while others may not—for instance, the saving of a child's life when the child would be condemned to a life of pain and suffering. This disagreement would show that people are either looking at the case in the light of different principles or that they hold opposite opinions as to whether a certain principle operates in this case or not. Those who would want to save the child's life whatever be the consequences would perhaps do so in recognition of the principle, 'life should be treated as possessed of value'. Those who would deny that the act of saving this child's life is right differ from others not through rejecting this principle as such but through limiting the scope of this principle in this particular case. They would argue that the value of life depends upon the requirement that there should be some possibility of happiness in a life; and a life bound to contain an excess of pain and suffering, with little or no pleasure, is lacking in this possibility. If one could be absolutely sure (as is unlikely)[1] that a particular life shows no promise of happiness whatsoever, one is justified in considering that the life concerned is not possessed of value.

The disagreement over this particular action then, although not a disagreement on principle as such, is a disagreement over the scope of a principle. This disagreement arises because some people consider the principle itself to be universally applicable, while others believe that the applicability of this principle should be judged in the light of the limit, consistency with which is the characteristic of the value point of view called morality, and this limit is that the value of life lies in the promise of happiness that it contains (the term happiness to be understood in a characteristic sense).

The validity of a moral principle, if it can be called a principle at all, is self-evident. If a contention is such that it can be questioned on general grounds (as distinct from questioning its scope in a particular case) we would hardly refer to it as a principle. A principle stands for a judgment as regards the suitability of a type of action to a feature (or features) in a situation whose nature is very broadly defined. Let us take, for instance, the principle 'a

---

[1] For a man condemned to a life of suffering may achieve a sense of personal worth through fighting against it and thus obtain a measure of happiness.

promise ought to be kept'. It says no more than that if anyone has undertaken to do something the doing of it is fitting to the situation which is constituted of the expectation that has been aroused in someone. It says nothing about the nature of the promise, the circumstances in which it has been made or has to be kept, the gravity of the adverse consequences that might follow the keeping of a promise and so on. But if we understand morality we understand that all these might make a difference to the keeping of a specific promise that has been made. The suitability that a principle embodies is thus a suitability of a general kind which has been conceived somewhat in abstraction from specific circumstances present in specific instances of promise-keeping.

Suppose that a particular situation is such that we consider that a particular promise ought not to be kept. If we just do not want to keep a promise we are not looking at the question morally. But if we are saying that a promise ought not to be kept in this case, we are making a moral judgment. And we cannot make a moral judgment without appealing to a standard which could justify our not keeping the promise. This standard can only be another principle which we find has greater authority in this case. I wish to suggest that whenever we are justified in considering that a certain principle is inapplicable in a certain case, the other principle whose authority we are accepting instead is a principle of a higher generality. We are justified in not keeping a promise if doing so would involve some appreciable damage to somebody or other's interests which we have no reason to think ought to be damaged, while the promise kept will not bring about a value of such a magnitude as will counter-balance the harm done. Thus our action in this particular case is in accordance with a principle of a greater generality and scope than the principle of truth-telling, namely 'be considerate to the needs and interests of other people'.

What then is involved in a principle being more general than another? By the degree of generality of a principle I mean the variety or types of actions that it can embrace. For instance, a highly general principle like 'be considerate etc.' can legislate in respect of a far greater variety of actions that an agent can perform than can the principle 'tell the truth'. Principles of action are in some way or other concerned with the satisfaction of human needs and calls. The more general a principle the less specific is the need in respect of which the principle prescribes a suitable action. Some needs are relatively specific and concrete in nature and a relatively definite type of activity fulfils it, like the need to be told the truth fulfilled by an activity involving verbal utterances of a characteristic kind. But a need like the need for recognition or for having one's interests respected does not appear in any particular form, nor is it that a definite type of activity fulfils or frustrates it. In fact, a need like this is a name that expresses the characteristic unity that there is between a variety of more specific needs. Thus, the more general principles include a variety of different types of needs rather than any one specific need or type of need in particular. Further, the more general a principle is the less we find it necessary to limit its scope. By the scope of a principle I mean something like this. The situations or features of situations with which principles deal are more or less specific. For instance, we can tell the truth only in that particular type of situation in which we are being asked for some information. But the situations in which we could be considerate are not of such a definite kind, nor do we have to do things of a particular type in order to be considerate. We can therefore think less of facts which limit the operation of a highly general principle like this than is the case with a less general principle, like the truth-telling one. Now there is a certain sense in which a more general principle is inclusive of a less general principle; for the abstract conception of a need in respect of which a highly general principle legislates constitutes an explanation of some sort of the relatively more specific types of needs in respect of which less general principles legislate. For instance, telling the truth is one way of respecting people and their interests, for the need to be told the truth is one amongst many needs which constitute a person's interest. Under normal circumstances, it happens that in respecting a principle of a lower generality we also respect a principle of a higher generality under which the former may in some ways be conceived. Only when these principles conflict, due to the complexity of prevailing circumstances, do we find it necessary to prefer a more general principle to a less general one.

A principle, of course, gains in generality and scope by being less directive of our particular actions in some sense, but to this I shall return later.

When we reflect on the highly general principles whose scope can far less be thought of as limited than is the case with the less general ones, it is easier for us to realize the limiting condition with which the conceptions of principles are found to be consistent on abstract considerations. This is the value that every human being has as an individual in his own right and Kant expressed this in the form of a law of morality (which he called 'the moral law', in its second formulation), namely 'treat every human being as an end in himself and never as a means only'. If every human being were a perfect moral agent and if nothing but what is one's duty was ever done, a situation of conflict between principles would never arise, as principles have been conceived consistently with the limiting condition of all moral actions. Conflict arises in actual situations because not everyone acts consistently with morality all the time. However, considering that conflict does exist, we may say that if the application of a principle in a particular case appears to violate the value that an individual has as an end (presuming that this violation is avoidable as far as morals is concerned), then the principle cannot be thought to be operative in the case. The reason why we find a rigid adherence to less general principles under all possible circumstances morally unsatisfactory is this. Less general principles prescribe in respect of relatively specific features of a situation. If we make it a rule to act on the relevant principle whenever such a feature is in evidence, we may overlook more general features, also present in the situation, in respect of which more general principles legislate. More general features being relatively abstract, their recognition usually proceeds along with the recognition of the value that an individual has for his own sake.

We are now in a position to define the concept of 'right' as the conception of principles which embody suitabilities of types of

actions to features of situations, when such actions are characterized by being consistent with the limit placed on our actions by
the value judgment 'every man is an end in himself'. Let us first
try to see what is involved in an individual's being an end in
himself before we discuss how this is involved in an individual's
recognition of a principle. To say that an individual is an end in
himself is to say that he is possessed of a certain value for his own
sake by virtue of certain characteristic differences that human
beings have from everything that is non-human. Now the thing
that is most valued by an individual in his life is happiness—in the
sense of a feeling of fulfilment and worth which produces joy and
gratefulness in being alive. Although such happiness cannot be
resolved into fulfilment of needs, it can come to exist only through
the fulfilment of certain needs (both physical, like the need for
food and warmth, and mental, like the need for recognition or for
creative activity and so on) felt by an individual and not through
their frustration. In order that there may be a sense of fulfilment
it is, of course, necessary that an individual should somewhat
organize his needs in order of relative importance in his own life,
and introduce a measure of harmony and integration between
them; for if the needs are warring between themselves the
satisfaction caused by the fulfilment of one will be cancelled
by the frustration of others. To treat human beings as ends in
themselves is to respect (unless there is a satisfactory reason why
one should not do it in a specific instance) whatever makes
possible the fulfilment of their various needs and calls and the
acquiring of worth in their own personalities.

Now to see what some of these principles are. Amongst the
principles that are highly general are principles concerning respect
and consideration for others, including respect for life, justice and
self-improvement. Under the principle of respect may be classified such principles as beneficence, non-malevolence, principles
related to general sympathy and friendliness, principles concerning the preservation of social forms, principles that operate
in the field of special relations and truth-speaking. Under the
heading of special relations come such principles as promise-
keeping, reparation, returning a benefit, filial gratitude, parental

and marital obligations and so on. Under justice come such principles as are related to the rejection of all inequalities in social, economic and political relations unless the presence of such inequalities can be justified on morally tenable grounds. And under self-improvement may be classified principles relating to self-control, courage, perseverance, self-collectedness and so on. (The conceptions of these principles show what a close relation there is between good attitudes and dispositions, and right principles, even though to talk about a right principle is not to talk about a good disposition.)

It is fairly obvious how these principles embody suitabilities of a moral nature. The requirement that we should in our actions have respect for other people and show consideration for their needs and interests is in accordance with the limiting condition of all moral actions, namely every man is an end in himself. If we disregard other people in our actions and show no concern for their possible needs and purposes that may be involved we treat them as if they are of no consequence. This is to violate the value that they have as individuals. The principle of justice which demands that nobody should be treated in a way that appears to be prejudicial or preferential, unless there are morally adequate reasons for doing so, is also consistent with this condition, for to treat anyone prejudicially is to assume that there is no need to recognize him as an individual in the same way as there is need to recognize the other who is given preference. The principle of self-improvement is also consistent with the requirement of morality, in as much as when we want to improve ourselves—in order that we may have as worthwhile a life as possible—we recognize our personalities as ends. For, if we have the ability to modify ourselves—as most of us believe that we have—so as to attain as much value in our own personality as we possibly can, it becomes our duty to do so in accordance with the law that we are ends in ourselves. For how can we be ends and yet not look for the best that life can offer us? As the less general principles may be classified under these in some ways there is no need to go into each to show that it is consistent with what may be called 'the moral law'.

We have said that in circumstances where a less general principle conflicts with a more general one, the more general one has a superior claim. But the more general a principle is the more abstract it is. That is to say, the less it says exactly what we should do. We may find ourselves in a situation in which we could not serve the legitimate interests of a person or of a group of people by observing the relatively concrete rules and principles that are recognized in a community. But there is no set way in which a highly abstract principle like serving the legitimate interests of people could be observed in the same manner in which the more concrete rules and principles could be observed. In such a case it is the agent who has to find out in the light of this principle a specific way of acting that fits the situation, and there is no guarantee that the way that he finds fits the case adequately. In ordinary circumstances of life, in paying respect to the relatively concrete and the more directly regulative principles we also pay respect to the more general and less directly regulative ones. In telling a person the truth we also respect his person and his legitimate needs and interests. But we become conscious of these abstract principles only when principles of a lower level conflict with them. This is only natural, as the higher-level principles are less directly regulative of our actions in the sense that they do not tell us exactly what we should do but merely give us a perspective from which we could choose. This latter point is true, of course, even of less general principles but in a lesser degree. A principle like 'tell the truth' is more directly regulative of our actions, for although it does not tell us exactly what we should say, it determines the conditions of our choice quite rigidly. But a principle like 'be considerate' determines our choice within a wider limit.

We have said that the more general a principle the less limited is its scope. But even a principle like 'do not harm or injure anybody' or 'be considerate to people's needs' may have its scope limited. One is justified in injuring another in self-defence, and when needs of different people conflict we have to choose some in preference to others which means that we cannot be considerate to some of the needs involved. The only maxim which is a categorical imperative in the sense that it cannot be violated without violating the point of view of morality is the law which defines the limit of moral activities, namely 'treat every man as an end in himself and never as a means only'. (This does not mean that nobody must ever be used as a means, only nobody should be used as a means only.)

Now to say that moral principles are hypothetical imperatives and it is only the moral law that is a categorical imperative is not to say any more than this: the scope of the moral law is not limited by anything, whilst that of the principles is limited by the law itself. If I am attacked violently by someone I am justified, in self-defence, in violating the principle 'do not harm or injure anybody', because it is necessary to maintain my status as an end which is being questioned by the attack. But I am not justified in injuring anyone more than is necessary to defend my status as an end, for if I do so, I injure his status as an end.[1] I am justified in violating a principle, then, if it conflicts with the limits imposed on our actions by the moral law. But so long as a principle remains consistent with the moral law its authority remains as categorical as that of the law itself.

Let us now try to see the relation between the law and the principles in a little more detail. I am afraid I can only attempt to clarify this relation by means of an analogy. The united kingdom called the British Isles is comprised of four different areas namely England, Scotland, Wales and Northern Ireland. The area or the country called England is again divided into smaller areas called counties, and a county in its turn is comprised of even smaller areas like boroughs and villages. A borough, say Beckenham, comes under the county of Kent, Kent under England, and England is a part of the British Isles. The British Isles in its turn is nothing but all the villages, boroughs, towns, counties, etc., of England, Scotland, Wales and Northern Ireland taken together. Now if we are saying something about Beckenham we are in a certain sense saying something about Kent, England and the

---

[1] If I am forced by circumstances to kill somebody in self-defence I injure his status as an end, and in that sense my action is morally wrong. But if I am not responsible for the circumstances being what they are I am exempt from moral blame.

British Isles. And anything that involves the whole of the British Isles involves England, Kent and Beckenham. But neither the British Isles nor Beckenham is a derivative of the other. Rather 'the British Isles' is the conception of an area which can be understood in greater and greater detail from some point of view as it is understood to be divided into smaller and smaller groups of local units. But a smaller group is nothing extraneous to the bigger group. To subdivide Kent into Beckenham, Bromley, etc., is not to add anything to the area of England when it is thought of merely in terms of counties. It is to understand the area of England in greater detail. Thus the relation between England and Kent and Kent and Beckenham is a relation between the sub-divisions of the same area and not between areas which exist as distinct localities independently of one another. The areas Beckenham and Kent co-exist, one being only a smaller division of the other and neither has Kent to exist before Beckenham nor Beckenham before Kent in order that Beckenham may be grouped under Kent. And although it is true to say that Beckenham is included in Kent, it is not the case that one must know Kent before one knows Beckenham. One might know Beckenham and subsequently come to know of the bigger division Kent. Or one might know Kent first and subsequently come to know that Beckenham is a borough in Kent. In short, our knowledge of Beckenham is not derived from our knowledge of Kent, nor is our knowledge of Kent derived from our knowledge of Beckenham. But our knowledge of Kent and that of Beckenham both belong to the conception of the same area, namely the British Isles, on different levels of local groupings.

Similarly, moral principles may be looked upon as manifestations of the same point of view, namely that of morality, but representing different levels in our conceptions of human needs and suitabilities of types of actions to features of situations involving such needs. A principle of a higher level then implies a principle of a lower level just as much as a principle of a lower level involves the principle of a higher level. To say that one principle is more general than another which is in some ways included in it is not to say that the less general is deduced from the more general, just as to say that Beckenham is a borough in Kent is not to deduce something from our knowledge of Kent. If Beckenham and places like it did not exist Kent would not exist either. In a similar way a principle like 'be considerate' could not be observed without observing lower-level principles like 'be truthful', 'keep a promise', etc. Again, if the principle 'be truthful' is properly understood as a moral principle it cannot be accepted without accepting a principle like 'be considerate'. Thus the traffic is not one way only, the deduction of the less from the more general, but it runs both ways—the implication of the more general in the less general and of the less general in the more general. The division of principles into more or less general is on the basis of the varieties of actions and types of needs that are involved, just as the classification of areas into counties or boroughs depends upon the extent of the localities involved.

It is no doubt true that when a less general principle is doubted we appeal to the authority of a more general principle which seems to back it up. One who would otherwise not keep a promise may be convinced about the moral appropriateness of promise-keeping by being told that if people in general refused to keep their promises social harmony will suffer. This might produce an impression that social harmony is the reason which justifies the keeping of a promise or that the justification of the principle of promise-keeping is deduced from that of social harmony. I am not denying that this might constitute a justification for keeping promises for somebody or other, but in what sense is this a justification? Why should the conception of social harmony appeal to one as morally authoritative when promise-keeping does not? If one would not dare disturb social harmony for fear of what might happen to one's own interests, one is acting on prudence and not on moral considerations. But if one is in such a frame of mind as to see the moral authority of the conception involved in social harmony, independently of what might happen to one's own self in case of harmony being disturbed, one would also see the moral point of promise-keeping independently of social harmony (without questioning, of course, that social harmony is morally desirable). Whatever authority a moral principle has it must have on its own back as a relatively concrete formulation of the moral law at a certain level of understanding concerning the suitability of a type of activity to certain features present in situations in which the satisfaction of human needs is involved and in which human beings may be treated as ends. A justification of a lower-level principle by a higher-level principle or by the moral law is thus not a deductive justification. The justification of a principle (if we should call it 'justification' at all, in view of the fact that the moral point of a principle—when it is evident—is self-evident) is a matter of giving it added support through clarification of its implications; it is not a process of making it acceptable through anything different from itself. If I decide not to harm somebody I was going to harm by being told that he is an end in himself, what has happened is not that additional information has justified the principle 'do not harm anybody' which I previously found to be unacceptable but that this principle has for the first time become a principle for me through a clarification of its implications. If I am bent upon harming somebody the piece of information that he is an end in himself will carry little weight, for this is what I am implicitly refusing to recognize or, at least, to act on by deciding to harm him.

The term 'right', we have said, may be applied to self-evident principles which are consistent with the moral law. That does not mean, however, that all the principles of a moral nature have already been formulated and that they are known to each and all. 'Self-evident' means 'self-justified' and not that they are already evident or evident to each and all. It may here be asked whether this self-evidence is logical or moral self-evidence. Let us accept that the general proposition 'murder is wrong' is a self-evident proposition. This would be logically self-evident only if we mean by 'murder' wrong killing. But then the proposition becomes a tautologous one. What the moral proposition asserts, however, is that the taking of another's life is wrong and not simply that when the taking of another's life is wrong, it is wrong. The moral self-evidence of a proposition is different from logical self-evidence when the word 'logical' is understood in a narrow sense. By the 'moral self-evidence' of a proposition is meant that the proposition is self-evident according to the *logic of moral reasoning*. To say that a particular reasoning is moral is to say that the reasoning in question is based on certain assumptions of the nature of standards of judgment—the assumptions being of such a nature that one feels justified in proceeding on their basis, as long as one is looking at the things concerned from a characteristic point of view. The most fundamental of these assumptions is that every individual is an end in himself, in the light of which it becomes evident that it is wrong to take the life of a human being, for to do so is to deny his status as an end in himself. 'It is wrong to take the life of a human being' is, then, a proposition that is morally self-evident (or evident according to the logic of moral reasoning) and not logically, the term 'logically' being understood in a narrow sense.

Now a principle stands for the suitability of a type of activity to a kind of situation or feature of situations involving human needs. As our experiences involving other people grow and the extent of our activities expands, new conceptions of suitabilities dawn upon us and sometimes a principle not yet thought of gets formulated on the occasion of a practical decision. It is not necessary that we must be consciously aware of the considerations on which we act before we can act in accordance with them. On the contrary it sometimes happens that we behave appropriately to a situation—and our behaviour shows that we do not doubt its appropriateness—without having consciously figured it out that the situation demands what it does and that the way in which we are behaving is the appropriate way. Take, for instance, the case of a man who steps on to the street from the pavement to cross the road; the sound of a horn makes him alert and he finds himself in danger of being run over by a car. Without stopping to think, the man steps back to the pavement. His action is appropriate to the situation, but most probably he has not consciously thought either (i) that he must save his life or (ii) that to save his life he must go out of the reach of the oncoming car. (Let us suppose that the incident has happened for the first time in the man's life so that it cannot be explained by habit.) But his behaviour leaves no doubt in our minds that he agrees with both (i) and (ii). This sort of behaviour has sometimes been referred to as an instance of wisdom of the body in order to distinguish it from the sort of behaviour which is consciously thought out as fitting to an accepted purpose. There is, of course, a danger in our talking of the 'wisdom of the body', for it might be taken to mean that our mind and body are two things somehow joined together to produce a man. But those who talk about this wisdom do not necessarily imply any bifurcation in the human personality. They may only wish to point out that human understanding and response belong to different levels of awareness and only at certain levels does this awareness become a conscious one. At levels lower than this we respond to situations in such a way that it may with justice be said that we understand the nature of the situation and the appropriateness of our behaviour to it, although we do not know consciously that we understand. Similarly it is possible that we sometimes understand the implications of a principle and the appropriateness of our behaviour to it at this lower level, which means that we are not able to formulate a principle even when we act in accordance with it. Thus it is justified to talk about a principle being implicit in our conduct even when it has not taken any definite shape in our conscious minds. Of course, our behaviour may be appropriate to a situation purely by accident. But when we consistently behave in a certain way in a certain type of situation it can fairly be said that we are acting on a principle in the sense that we are implicitly agreeing with it in our conduct. It is then not necessarily the case that all the moral principles that we may refer to by the term 'right' have definitely been formulated or that a principle to be a principle must be known to all as a verbalized formula. As human situations grow or change, new suitabilities that may form the content of principles may arise which are at first recognized at a lower level and only subsequently consciously formulated.

Now what exactly is involved in our respecting a principle? It can hardly be the case that we begin with an abstract principle

M

irrespective of any particular situation that we may be in and do what it says is right. We do what is suitable to a particular situation here and now without stopping to think what sort of a principle is relevant to it and what follows from that principle. Rather, a principle may be read out of our actual behaviour when we continue to act in some consistent manner. There are times, of course, when an agent does not know what action in particular or sort of action suits the situation present. He might then consciously adopt a principle which somehow appears to be relevant and see what sort of action would be in accordance with it in this particular case. But the abstract and general nature of a principle gives him no more than a guidance in approaching the issue of deliberation. It does not so much deliver a definite conclusion as help the agent towards finding one by eliminating some possible courses of conduct which are definitely found to be not in accordance with it. The logical force of a general principle lies mainly in this, that it can lead the agent to reject some possible or proposed actions as being unsuitable to the situation as viewed morally. How much we positively get out of a principle depends upon the complexity of the situation. But there is no doubt that a principle is a positive conception of a suitability and it orients us in certain directions rather than in others.

Finally, does it or does it not do us any good to be taught general principles of morals? General principles have no more than a broad regulative function in determining what we should actually do. They might lead us to reject certain possible ways of behaving towards which we feel impelled, as contrary to the conceptions of morally suitable actions. But they only provide a framework within which deliberations and decisions regarding what we should do may take place. It has sometimes been objected that the teaching of fixed principles makes our minds rigid, and rigidity is fatal to creative morality; and after all is said and done, the only morality that is practically important is morality that is creative. If we are taught certain fixed principles from which we are to deduce our duties we are being taught to forego our individual judgments and decisions in favour of a set pattern. Life is too complex and too much in a flux to be tied down to patterns. There is much truth in this objection, but it is not fatal to principles that are highly general and abstract. If it is true that a principle like 'be considerate to others' gives a certain pattern to our behaviour, it is equally true that there is ample scope for creative moves within the limits of the pattern. Indeed, there is a certain sense in which this principle demands that we should be creative, for it is nothing but a formal statement of a suitability to which a content is given by our decisions. A general principle does not at all tell us what exactly we should do, only it tells us (leaving extreme cases aside) whether that which we think we should do is not morally unsuitable to the situation involved. We can thus adopt certain general principles and at the same time retain our individual initiative and judgment.

There is yet another objection to the teaching of principles which I find has a great deal of truth in it. A child may be taught the abstract principle 'be considerate', but it remains an empty verbiage so long as he has not had lots of experiences in which he is in a position either to fulfil or frustrate other people's needs and interests and so long as he does not learn from actual practice the distinction between the type of action that shows considera- tion and the type of action that does not. A principle like 'be considerate' becomes a principle only through one's actually learning to be considerate in the practical business of life. That is to say, a child does not become considerate by hearing 'be considerate' independently of any context of action. One comes to adopt this principle, if one does, because one has learnt through practical conflicts of life to be considerate. This I think is largely true; there is no short cut to morality, at least to morality in the world known to us. One comes to realize—and it is a matter of realization and not merely of knowledge in the sense of being informed—what is right by doing what is right and perhaps doing also what is wrong and in coming to see the distinction between the two in practical experience. It is hardly conceivable that a child could be made into a saint merely by the passing over of certain verbal information about the requirements of morality, and as far as practical understanding goes it only comes through wide personal contact with both good and evil, right and wrong. In order that this practical understanding may take place a child has to be left with some room to grow as an individual person and given opportunities to take personal decisions even though some of the disasters that result from it could be avoided if others decided on his behalf. And this remains the only way to learn to act morally.

In spite of all these considerations, however, principles are not reduced to useless fictions. They retain their significance as the logical implicates of certain types of conduct when these are looked at morally—conduct that we actually know of and conduct that we think could or should exist. Moreover, they have a certain practical significance of an important kind. Although it is true that a principle becomes a principle only when we have learnt to act in accordance with it, it is not true that our coming to learn to act in accordance with it may not be helped in some ways through a process of teaching. A child must teach himself to be considerate, but his self-teaching may be made considerably easier by his being told to be considerate on appropriate occasions. Further, our adherence to a principle may be of different degrees, particularly to principles that are highly general. Most of us are often pulled in different directions, and although we may recognize the authority of a principle in general, its demand may be too high for us to want to obey it in any particular case. The reiteration of a principle, even when it is nothing new to us, often adds to the hold that it actually has over us by bringing it to the centre of our attention.

I shall now turn to the concept of 'duty'. When understood to be distinguishable from the concept of 'right' it refers to particular acts most suitable from the point of view of morality to particular situations in which an agent is called upon to act. Particular situations of life are specific in nature and they may show the relevance of more than one principle. Moreover, if a situation is very complex, the precise features in it that are morally relevant may not be obvious. It is therefore incumbent on us to try to understand the concrete character of a situation before we can proceed to act in a manner that is prescribed by a principle. Instead of its being the case that we deduce our duties from self-evident principles of morals, normally to see that a principle is operative in a particular case is to see what is our duty. I said normally, for we are not under an obligation to do whatever a principle says is right whenever a principle is recognized to be relevant in any particular case. What is right—the term being used in the sense of a principle—has been termed by Ross a 'prima facie duty or obligation'. A general conception of right stands for the suitability of a type of action X to a characteristic feature Y found in a situation. If one is in a situation which shows feature Y one is, on the face of it, under an obligation to perform X; and this obligation stands unless the situation shows other features as well which confer on us a different obligation. It is thus not necessarily the case that we are under an obligation to perform any particular action whenever we recognize that a principle is relevant in a particular case, for the obligation may be no more than a prima facie one. The action that is actually binding on us is one that is suitable to the total situation as viewed morally and not merely to any particular feature of it, if the total situation shows more than one morally relevant aspect. It can, therefore, be said that we cannot and do not deduce our duties from general principles. A rule (principle) can only be abstract, while a particular act must have a concrete character to fit a concrete situation. So it will always be necessary to satisfy ourselves that a situation fits in completely within the conception of an abstract moral feature before we act on a principle, and for this no rule can be given.

What function, then, do principles play in the determination of our duties if we do not deduce these from the principles? As I have already remarked, as far as unambiguous instances are concerned to see our duty is to recognize a principle and to recognize a principle is to see our duty, and there are not two successive steps involved from one to the other. But in ambiguous instances we do not see plainly wherein our duty lies, and it becomes necessary for us to appeal to a general principle. Here a principle is accepted as a standard (i.e. we wish to respect the conception of moral suitability that is embodied in a principle; for instance, we may wish to do justice to an individual or to a

group) in the light of which the situation is approached. This
orients us towards singling out those features of the situation
which particularly bear upon it, and these when considered fully
—after due weight is given to other features, of course—may lead
us towards a particular action which fits these features as well as
it is possible under the circumstances. A principle, then, acts as a
standard in the light of which we approach the question of our
duty, when we do not see our duty directly. Again, when we
wish to judge whether a particular action performed fits the
situation as well as it is possible for an action to fit it morally, it
is the conception of a principle (or conceptions of principles)
that acts as the standard of evaluation. Much of the controversy
in Ethics as regards the self-evident nature of what is right may
be traced to a confusion between the concept of 'right' in its
general significance and the concept of 'duty' which stands for
what is right in a particular case, or to put it in another way,
between 'duty' which is another name for 'right' in general and
'duty' which refers to something that is right in particular. When
Kant says that we must do our duty come what may and proceeds
to talk of our duties in general terms, like our duty to tell the
truth and so on, a difficulty is created because of Kant's refusal to
make a distinction between 'duty' which means a particular
action which fits a particular situation and 'duty' which means
the general suitability of a type of action to a certain feature in a
situation. What is right in a particular case, i.e. what is one's duty,
seldom has the self-evidence which what is right in general has.
In fact, what is one's duty is never self-evident unless the particular case is so simple as to show no other moral relevance than
that of a feature which fits in completely within the conception
of a general type. But controversies about duty arise in cases
which are complex (i.e. which show the relevance of more than
one principle) and there it is as important to exercise one's own
judgment in accepting one principle in preference to another and
in determining the moral nature of the situation in accordance
with it as to pay respect to the prima facie obligations involved
in the conceptions of standards. The rigorism of Kant's moral
theory could be avoided if he distinguished 'right' from 'duty'

and made it clear that the impossibility of questioning the rightness of what is right belongs to the plane of abstract thought about general suitabilities.

Here it is useful to compare the formulation of a principle with that of a law in physics. A law in physics can only be formulated in terms that are unconditional, it cannot be expected to include all the limitations that exist in practice on its operations. Let us take, for instance, Snell's Law—the ratio of the sines of the angle of incidence and refraction is constant. There are certain substances which do not behave in the way the law suggests, but these are not specifically mentioned in the body of the law itself. As Toulmin puts it, '"Most transparent substances of uniform density, excluding only certain crystalline material such as Iceland Spar, have been found to refract light in such and such a manner" is not what we call Snell's Law'. But a law does not become invalid if it is found that it is inapplicable to certain things under certain circumstances. A principle, likewise, is a general statement of a suitability which cannot be questioned so long as we are talking about the conception involved in this general statement. What can be questioned is the application of a principle to a particular case. That is to say, in so far as a principle is applicable, its applicability in relation to a characteristic approach to an issue needs no support, which is another way of saying that it is self-evident. It is therefore a truism to say that no exception to a principle can exist so long as we have in mind merely the character of a principle; but although a truism, it is a valid statement. But when it comes to an actual situation, it is possible to find that the scope of a principle somehow relevant to the situation is yet limited to this particular case because of such and such factors also present in the case which are not catered for in the principle. We cannot therefore agree with Kant that it is always our duty to tell the truth whenever in concrete situations of life we are asked by anybody about something or other. Yet the principle 'tell the truth' remains a self-evident general principle.

It is no doubt true that we are all apt to find good reasons for making an exception to a principle in our own case, and perhaps by referring to some principles as duties of perfect obligation Kant had it in mind that very often the justifications that are sought for violating an obligation of this kind are not acceptable from the point of view of morality. This is why the term 'prima facie obligation' suits the case so admirably. Our obligation to act in a way which is recommended by a principle (relevant to the situation) stands, unless a counter-obligation of even greater authority requires us to act contrary to it. Admittedly it is not as easy to form an adequate decision in such matters as it sounds on paper; yet the difficulties may perhaps be unduly magnified, particularly because a moral act may make very exacting demands on some of the inclinations an agent may naturally feel. In any case, the obligation to follow a principle is 'prima facie' as suggested by Ross and not unconditional as Kant thinks.

Now the term 'prima facie obligation' is a term that has been called by Strawson 'a deceptively helpful notion'. The deception possibly lies in this. Suppose someone says 'I have an obligation to do X', meaning an action which actually is his duty. If questioned how he knows that he is obliged to do X the man may say that he knows it because the existence of the circumstances of the kind P (which is what the existing circumstance is) entails an obligation of the kind X, or in other words because he has a prima facie obligation to do X. Here it looks as if the man has given an explanation of how he has discerned his duty. But, says Strawson, the knowledge of particular obligations (or Obligations as Strawson would put it) is a pre-condition of any knowledge of prima facie obligation (or obligation as Strawson would put it). To say therefore that one knows X to be one's duty because one knows that X constitutes a 'prima facie' obligation is to put the cart before the horse. One knows one's obligations (i.e. prima facie obligations) because one knows one's Obligations. To suppose that one knows one's Obligations because one knows one's obligations is to be deceived by the term 'prima facie'.

Now which do we know first, obligation or Obligation? I suspect there is a confusion in the very posing of the question itself. It seems to me that under ordinary circumstances, when we do not have any doubt as regards what is our duty (particular obligation or Obligation), there are not two distinct processes, one of discerning a prima facie obligation and another of deducing a particular obligation from it. For to see that *X* is one's duty in the situation *Y* is to recognize implicitly that *X* is a type of action that fits the type of features that are morally relevant in situation *Y*—if by the word 'duty' is meant a moral act and not merely an act one is personally disposed to undertake. Here there is no question therefore of deducing one from the other. The matter, however, becomes complicated when we do not see our duty directly. Let us suppose that the situation in which we are called upon to act is *Y* and we do not know what to do, not because we do not find any morally relevant aspect in it but because there is more than one morally relevant aspect and the actions required by these aspects oppose one another in some ways. What we have to do in such a case is to analyse the situation in order to see as clearly as possible its various morally relevant aspects. Let us suppose these aspects are *p, q, r*. When we have come to this stage we may find that *p* is such that it confers on us the obligation to do *m, q, n*, and *r, o*. Since we can only do one of these acts (suppose that this is so) it cannot be said that *m, n, o* are our obligations but it is perfectly sensible to say that they represent prima facie obligations (i.e. they appear to be obligations when certain features of a situation are considered). Now suppose further that we find *p* to be the most urgent or important moral aspect of the situation, then our prima facie obligation to do *m* becomes an actual obligation. The process of thinking that is involved in this deliberation is, of course, not deductive. To say '*m* is my duty here and now because I have a prima facie obligation to do *m* whenever a feature of the sort *p* is the most prominent moral feature in a situation' is not to deduce anything from anything. It is to support a particular apprehension of duty—if such a support is needed—by saying that the undertaking of what one is proposing to undertake means respecting a principle (a prima facie obligation) that ought to be respected in this case, inasmuch as this principle recommends an action that is morally most fitting to the situation, under the circumstances. This sort of thinking or reasoning does not fit in with either inductive or deductive reasoning, the only two types of reasoning that are usually recognized as logical. The reason appears to me to be this. Inductive and deductive processes are processes of reasoning appropriate for the consideration of non-value facts, something more is needed for a process of reasoning which is evaluative. For every act of evaluation proceeds in the light of a standard—implicit or explicit—and the function of thinking in evaluation consists in showing the relevance of a particular standard in a case—a standard which would either justify itself or can be shown to be ultimately backed by something which justifies itself. This sort of reasoning has a logic of its own and this logic operates once we have accepted the standard involved, yet it cannot be put down to any definite logical pattern.

Although our particular duties cannot be looked upon as deductions from general principles, principles play an important regulative part in the determination of duties in so far as a man adopts the point of view of morality. To adopt the point of view of morality is to act in conformity with certain very general conceptions as to the value of human beings as individuals and as to the sorts of human behaviour that fit in with this supposed value of individuals as persons in situations showing certain characteristic features. Of course, the part these general conceptions play can only be regulative, i.e. they tell us that certain sorts of actions will be inconsistent with the point of view of morality in certain situations rather than directly inform us of a particular action that fits a particular situation. But in so far as a man adopts the point of view of morality he accepts the regulative authority of these conceptions, with which his own considerations as to what is his duty are required to be in accord. Also he accepts that if it becomes necessary to question one's estimation of duty, it is the conceptions of these principles which provide one with the standard, either implicit or explicit, of a value judgment in this respect. Inasmuch as the point of view of morality is an impartial point of view—a point of view from which one looks at oneself and not only at others as an impartial spectator—it may be said that it is more reasonable that a human being should adopt this point of view than that he should not.

Now we have said that the concept of 'duty' applies to particular actions that are morally most suitable to particular situations. But when we apply the concept of 'duty' we also mean that some agent or other is obliged to act in that particular way which is morally most suitable to the situation. The question of duty arises in situations in which certain changes need to be effected. One has then to understand certain things about the persons and things involved in a situation, the features that need to be changed as well as the changes that need to be brought about. Moreover, one has to be reasonably certain of the consequences that will follow one's acting in a certain way. All these give rise to a certain difficulty. In view of the fact that moral situations are often complex, it cannot be expected that everyone would have the same opinion about the moral nature of a situation and about what is suitable to it. It is by no means always the case that a man, however virtuous he may be, has a full grasp of the nature of a situation or of the consequences that will actually follow an action. In fact nobody can visualize all the consequences that will follow an action, except in cases which are very simple and straightforward. To say then that a man is obliged to do that which is most suitable to a situation is to demand the impossible. A man cannot be obliged to do what he cannot do and often a man does not know beforehand that a particular action is the most suitable to a situation. It has therefore been held that obligation is subjective and not objective. That is to say, a man is obliged to do not what the real situation really demands but what the agent thinks is demanded by the situation whose nature he seriously supposes to be of a certain kind. A man cannot be obliged, says Ross, to act in relation to situation X, supposing that X expresses the real nature of the situation, if he sincerely believes that the situation demanding an action from him is of the nature Y. Again, a man cannot do P, which is what the situation really demands, if he seriously believes that the situation demands Q. We do not believe, says Ross, that a man acts rightly if he acts contrary to his convictions even if by so acting he accidentally produces the results that are desirable. Again, we do not blame a man for doing P, if he seriously believes that the doing of *P* is his duty even if the consequences of doing *P* are not desirable. Ross admits that the objective view is in some ways implied in the way we use the concepts of 'duty' and 'obligation'. But he says that it is subjective rightness that is ethically more important. And consequently one's obligation is obligation to do what one thinks one ought to do.

I think that subjective rightness is ethically important. Its recognition is based on the recognition of the personal character of the responsibility that a moral agent has in undertaking an action. A man cannot be held properly responsible for his actions unless he acts on personal (i.e. subjective) conviction. To demand that a man must do what is objectively right whether or not he believes it to be right is an impossible demand. But it is objective in another sense. A man's personal opinion is not necessarily adequate, and quite often it leaves scope for improvement. As far as morals is concerned there is always an obligation on a man to keep before him the objective ideal of a most suitable action as well as to endeavour to approximate to it as far as possible. The excuse 'I did not know it to be my duty' does not always exempt a man from moral blame but it would do so if obligation is nothing but subjective. I do not therefore think that subjective rightness is ethically the more important. Rather, objective rightness is the ideal which an agent in his subjective approach to what is right is obliged to respect as far as it is possible for him to do so.

The next question to be asked is, 'What exactly is it that we are obliged to do?' An act, says Ross, is the production of a change in a state of affairs or, as in comparatively few cases, maintenance of a state of affairs which also involves change in some ways, in so far as the state of affairs will not be maintained without the act. Now the only changes we can directly produce are changes in our body or mind. But, says Ross, in his *The Right and the Good* these are not as such what as a rule we think is our duty to produce. Ross takes a simple act like fulfilling the promise of returning a book to a friend. Suppose that one decided to return it by post. Between the packing and posting of the book and the receiving of that by the friend there intervenes a series of occurrences. The utilitarian would say that our duty is to act in a certain way, e.g. pack and post the book, so as to produce a certain consequence, e.g. the receiving of the book by the friend. But, says Ross, it is not the packing and posting that is our duty. Our duty is to fulfil our promise, i.e. put the book in our friend's possession. One's act is right not qua the packing and posting of a book but qua the securing of the friend's receiving the book. If the friend does not get the book because of certain intervening occurrences it still remains one's duty to secure one's friend another copy. Thus an act is right qua being an ensuring of one of the particular states of affairs of which it is an ensuring, namely, in the case we have taken, of the friend's receiving the book he has been promised. The packing and posting are right only incidentally. It is not the case that our duty is to do certain things, packing and posting, which will produce a certain result, receiving of the book. Our duty is to ensure the receiving of the book by the friend, i.e. to fulfil our promise.

Ross gives a somewhat different account of which we are obliged to do in *Foundations of Ethics*. There it appears that instead of its being our duty to secure that our friend gets the book our duty is to set ourselves to bring the receiving about. But setting ourselves to do something is to produce some changes in our body and mind which is not what Ross thinks is our duty as such in *The Right and the Good*. This modified view, as far as I can make out, comes rather near the utilitarian view, namely, our duty is to do something (in this case, to set ourselves) to bring about a certain result (the receiving of the book). There is, of course, an important difference; while according to the utilitarian view what is our duty to do—in order that a certain result may be brought about—may be of many different kinds, depending upon the kind of result that is to be brought about, Ross and Prichard would say that what is our duty is always the same, namely, to set ourselves to do something.

The substitution of 'setting ourselves to bring about some result' for 'bringing about some result', Ross believes, helps one to decide in favour of the subjective view of duty. But this account does not seem to me quite satisfactory. There is, of course, a certain plausibility in saying that our obligation is an obligation to set ourselves to do a certain thing. For unless we do so no action would follow. Further, this is what we are directly capable of doing, while the state of affairs we intend to bring about comes about relatively indirectly. But it does not seem to me that we need conceive of our 'obligation to set ourselves to do something' and 'our obligation to bring about a certain state' as contraries, so that a substitution of one by the other is called for. Rather, these two obligations are two aspects of the same task, namely, the doing of our duty—one is the aspect of doing something to ourselves with a view to start ourselves off as agents, and the other is that of effecting a certain change in the existing state of affairs. As Ross himself says, even if we had set ourselves to bring about that our friend gets the book we have promised to return to him by packing and posting it and our friend does not receive it due to an accident in the post-office, we are still under an obligation to secure him another copy. The only difference that the modified view makes is this. An agent who had set himself to bring about that the friend gets the books is thereby *free of blame*, irrespective of whether the friend actually gets the book or not. It still remains the agent's duty to secure the receiving of the book by the friend, but he is not blameworthy for his friend's not having received it already, as he would be if he had not sent it at all. If the agent has done his duty only when the friend has actually received the book and not when he has carefully packed and posted it, believing his action to be the most fitting to the requirement that his friend gets the book in time, it cannot be believed that obligation is purely subjective. A man will have done his duty when he has sent a book off by post if he thinks that this is the best possible means of securing the receiving of the book by his friend, whether or not his friend actually gets it— if we believe that a man's duty does not go beyond setting himself to do what he thinks is the most fitting to a supposed situation. If the ideal of duty be the doing of what fits the situation, there is a sense in which it must be said that the agent's obligation is rooted in the objective facts of the situation, although there are circumstances where this ideal can only be realized more or less and in which it is possible only to think that a certain action fits the situation and not know it with any degree of certainty.

As to the dispute between Ross and the utilitarians regarding whether it is our duty to do something to bring about a certain good result or to produce a certain state of affairs. On the face of it there seems to be little difference between saying that it is our duty to pack and post a book in order to produce the result that our friend gets it and that it is our duty to secure the receiving of the book by our friend through such activities as packing and posting of the book. They appear to be two alternative ways of saying the same thing as far as a particular instance of duty is concerned. But, says Ross, there is a difference, and as far as I can see the difference is a difference of implications. According to the utilitarian account an act is right because of the goodness of the consequences that are produced by it. It is then the action consisting in the packing and posting of the book that is right and its rightness belongs to it because of the good result that it brings about, namely, that the friend gets the book and is satisfied—or would normally be satisfied. This way of putting the thing may be quite harmless as long as the situation demanding a certain kind of action from us is comparatively simple. But as soon as the situation begins to be complex and a straightforward connection between a particular action and certain results cannot be seen with certainty determination of our duties becomes impossible (for our duty is to do that which will bring about a certain good result). Moreover, if in a complex case we feel somewhat sure (which is different from saying that we know) that a certain course of action will bring about a certain good result we may embark on the course of action thinking only of the result that we think is going to follow and not at all of the character of the action itself. Ross's account has this advantage over the utilitarian one in such cases that an act has to be understood as right because of what it is, i.e. because of its own character as the bringing about of a state of affairs and not because of some results understood as its consequences as distinct from the act itself. In other words, when we have to decide on a particular action as the right one in a complex situation, it will not do, as far as morality is concerned, to hit upon any action which we think will give rise to certain consequences we accept as good—this would have done if we understood the 'rightness' of an action merely in terms of good consequences—what we have also to consider is the character of the act itself as an integral part in the bringing about of a state of affairs, the bringing about of which in a certain situation constitutes, in some ways, an obligation on the part of an agent. To take a concrete example. X has promised Y to be present at a party given by him on a certain evening. Due to an unexpected offer X gets a free ticket in the same evening for an opera which he had wanted to see but had not been able to afford. The pleasure that he would get out of his visit to the opera is very much more than the pleasure that he himself or his friend would get out of his presence at the party. We cannot even say that the disappointment caused to the friend by his absence would be of a great magnitude. If we are to decide in terms of good consequences we shall have to say that the act of paying a visit to the opera would be the right act. But if we are to think of our duty as the bringing about of a state of affairs which ought to be brought about, then clearly the act of going to the party would be the right act, inasmuch as by so doing he will bring about a state of affairs which he ought to bring about— namely, the fulfilment of his promise. The mere fact of a promise being made confers on one the responsibility of keeping that promise and an action is right as the fulfilling of that responsibility quite apart from any particular good result that might follow. The utilitarian might say that it is the fulfilment of the promise that is the good result to be produced in this case. But if the pleasure and over-all benefit produced by X's going to the opera is greater than those produced by his going to the party, then to say that the fulfilment of the promise is the good consequence that ought to be brought about in preference to the pleasure and benefit to be derived by X from going to the opera is already to choose a good consequence in terms of something which involves more than a consideration of consequences. It is already to recognise the prior claim of promise-keeping as the fulfilment of an obligation that an agent has, even when it does not lead to greater pleasure. It is possible for the utilitarian to say in reply that the general fulfilling of promises is essential for human happiness and although the fulfilment of this particular promise would not lead to greater happiness a failure to fulfil it will contribute to the weakening of the general practice of promise-keeping in society. But suppose that none but the friend whose devotion to moral principles is genuine (which means that he may reasonably be expected not to follow the example of his friend) knows of this promise being made, and the fact that this promise has been broken will not be known to anyone else. In a case like this we need not fear that the breaking of this promise will lead to the weakening of the practice of promise-keeping and the utilitarian reply would not cover it.

A few more words before I close this chapter on 'duty'. The concept of 'duty' is, from the practical point of view, the most important and the most fundamental in morals. Moral problems arise with the asking of questions like 'What should be done about this?' or, 'Should this have been done or avoided?' It is only in course of answering these questions that we come upon the concepts of 'right' and 'good' which we find provide us with standards in terms of which we could proceed to answer the questions asked. But these questions are also the most difficult ones to answer. The mere fact that a question is asked shows that the answer is not evident. But the nature of the conceptions that can be referred to by 'right' and 'good' in their capacity as standards is evident. But they are abstract and general conceptions which do not fully cater for the concrete nature of all particular instances of action. This confers on us the responsibility of exercising our individual judgment and discretion in our approach to individual issues, although, of course, in accordance with a characteristic point of view from which human beings are supposed to have a certain value for their own sakes and which requires that we should treat them in certain ways whenever certain features involving human needs are involved (these ways are embodied in the conceptions of virtues and principles). We must then have a degree of intelligence in order to discern,

N

if we are at all able to do so, what our duties are. A moral agent is thus responsible not only for respecting principles but also for making an intelligent approach to the question of what should be done in circumstances of a specific kind. In the last resort, it is on this that the doing of our duties hangs, provided we possess the disposition called 'conscientiousness' which orients us towards the doing of our duties. Philosophy cannot solve the practical problems of moral behaviour, for there is no set solution to be had. It can only clarify our ideas in terms of which we approach a problem at hand and thus can contribute in a round-about way towards the finding of a solution, if and when we do find a solution to a complicated problem; or, which is equally important, if there is no 'solution' to be had, towards the realization that the question can have no solution in the ordinary sense of the term.

CHAPTER VIII

Moral Praise and Blame

It is sometimes argued that human behaviour is determined by genetic constitution, social environment, glandular secretions and so on, and this being the case judgments of praise and blame are out of place. There are many interesting and important questions to be asked on this topic but I can only touch upon them here as briefly as possible.

We know that there is some relation between a man's genetic constitution and his achievement. That is to say, given a certain genetic constitution we could perhaps say (supposing that our knowledge in such matters is sufficiently precise, which is doubtful) that there are certain things that are beyond the power of the man concerned, while certain others are not. But our knowledge of a man's genetic constitution does not allow us to say that he must act in such and such particular ways, or do such and such particular things. Moral choice is usually exercised over such issues (the issue is of this type, 'Shall I or shall I not keep this promise?' or 'This man is a foreigner, and he does not know the price of this article; shall I or shall I not charge him more?') that no particular type of genetic constitution is presupposed in order that a choice may be exercised at all, and a man with a given constitution is not bound to decide one way or the other except in some restricted cases. For instance, a man who is constitutionally so weak that he could not learn to swim cannot reasonably be expected to jump into a river to rescue a drowning man. Of course, moral behaviour presupposes a degree of intelligence—and intelligence is usually recognized to be an inherited (i.e. a congenital) ability—referred to as average or normal intelligence;

and people who may be supposed to be below normal intelligence cannot be expected to make a satisfactory moral decision except when it is fully covered by habit. It is possible again that glandular over- or under-secretion makes it impossible for people to exercise any control over their own behaviour and such people should be recommended for medical treatment rather than for moral condemnation. But allowance is normally made in our moral judgments for people with physiological and glandular deficiency and abnormality if such deficiency and abnormality are known to exist; and if not made it should be made. When we praise or blame people we presuppose that the people concerned are normal; and as far as these people are concerned, in whatever way they may be determined by their constitution such determination is not fatal to the possibility *of all moral choice.* Admittedly, it is not always easy to determine whether a person is normal in this sense or not. This shows, not that our judgments of praise or blame should all be scrapped, but that we must take care to find out whether a man's failures are due to any constitutional limitation, and in case it is we must refrain from blaming him. Further, as we cannot always be sure whether a man may not be suffering from a constitutional limitation of some degree, we should keep an open mind when we blame people and be willing to reverse our judgment if any evidence of an inherited inability may be forthcoming. It may be said to this that no such evidence may be forthcoming and yet people may be limited in this way. I would say in reply that the only reason to think that a man is limited in this way is provided by actual evidences to this effect. We have no justification for thinking that a man is limited in this way if no evidence is ever come across, although we must admit the possibility that a man may be so limited, which means that we should be willing to change our mind about him if a reason is furnished. The onus of establishing that a man is limited or subnormal lies on the one who contests the idea that he is normal, whereas one is normally justified in believing another person to be normal, unless there are reasons one knows of to believe the contrary. There is, of course, an element of risk in this, for at no stage do we know enough about a person to be absolutely sure and no doubt we make mistakes about people. Even so, it is more reasonable to believe that a person is normal when we are not possessed of any reason to think that he is not than to believe that he is not without any evidence to establish our belief.

Let us now consider sociological determination. Human behaviour, particularly behaviour that is morally relevant, is certainly influenced to a great extent by sociological factors. Most of us are taught from our early childhood to do things that are usually approved of in the society we live in and not to do things that are disapproved of. As a result of such training, pro-attitudes to certain ways of behaving and aversion to certain others become almost a second nature to us and we do or avoid things without thought. It is hardly possible to deny this fact today; but the question is: if a certain habit of acting or not acting in a certain way is found—at a certain stage of social development—to conflict with the requirements of morality is it or is it not possible for us, in principle, to break through the habit? If we look at the history of any human society that has progressed beyond the most primitive stage we shall find that it is possible, at least on the part of some people; otherwise social development could hardly have taken place. Perhaps it is true that only people who are exceptional in some ways can do so. But ordinary people who belong to the same society do not blame one another for behaving in ways that are socially approved of. And people who have greater vision in the same society or people belonging to other societies should not consider anyone blameworthy for behaving in a way that is approved of in the society he belongs to (unless the person is recognizable as exceptional in a requisite way) however much they think that the way in question is morally unsatisfactory and should be changed. People in general should not be blamed for doing what is usually done even when what is generally done ought not to be done under certain changed circumstances. For the ability to see that what is generally done may yet be wrong is an exceptional ability and it should not be presumed to exist equally in all. But judgments of praise and blame can still hold within the limits of sociological determination, for it is not necessarily the case that we always do what our society approves of.

Let us now consider psychological determination. Our choice of actions certainly depends to a great extent upon the sort of persons we already are at the moment of choice, i.e. upon our existing attitudes, dispositions and character. Our attitudes, dispositions, and character grow almost imperceptibly through an interplay of many different factors, some being of the nature of innate tendencies, others arising from particular circumstances; they do not come to exist as a result of a plan consciously made by ourselves. Besides, we have no say in the matter of what natural tendencies we shall feel or what circumstances we shall be in, particularly in our formative years, after which we are more or less made. How can we then be blamed for our actions which ultimately depend on conditions that are very little or not at all under our control?

Now it is not to be denied that our actions are usually causally related to the attitudes, etc., that we already possess, and that usually our attitudes develop without our knowing about them. But the important question for our purposes is: 'Is it or is it not possible for us to change our hitherto existing tendencies if we find that our tendencies are not morally satisfactory?' Its eems to me to be beyond doubt at least some people can do so, in which case psychological determinism fails as a theory that can rule out the possibility of all moral choice whatsoever for anyone. Although we are usually unaware of the tendencies and attitudes that orient us in certain directions, it is possible for us to come to know of their presence—we may come upon them ourselves or we may be told by other people and subsequently recognize them—in crucial instances of conflict of obligations or conflict of obligation with inclination. And once we recognize them it is possible for us, theoretically at any rate, to try to resist the hold they have on our choice; and if it is not guaranteed that we shall succeed, neither is it guaranteed that we shall fail. Of course, people are more or less determined by their psychological past. Some people are so embedded in their existing mental habits that it is beyond their intellectual power to consider that it may be necessary to look at these habits critically. Their habitual behaviour (i.e. behaviour which is, to begin with, learnt) takes on more and more the shape of impulsive or instinctive behaviour. And as this happens they become almost incapable even of thinking of resisting it. Therefore there is a certain plausibility in saying that these people can no longer be considered to be moral agents in respect of such behaviour and they should not be blamed for what they do. No doubt this is true of some people. It is also true that most of us cannot be expected to take the initiative to find out our undesirable traits, for whatever becomes habitual with us is taken for granted and does not any longer arouse any question. But we are sometimes told of our undesirable traits by people who do not like us and sometimes even by those who do like us, and then it can no longer be said that we cannot change our attitudes because we are unaware of them. Of course, some people find it hard or even impossible to believe that their attitudes may in any way need changing even when their unsatisfactory character is pointed out to them. Maybe in this they are determined, but I am inclined to think that one can only be determined in this by a sense of exaggerated self-importance which all of us are tempted to feel and which blinds us to any of our possible imperfections. But must we accept this import-ance as an ultimate fact, simply because it is in some sense natural for us to feel it, or is it that normally speaking (normally, because a sense of exaggerated self-importance may be a symptom of some pathological condition) it is possible for us to learn to limit this importance by the importance of whatever lies beyond us?

It must, of course, be admitted here that the task is not an easy one and that how far one is able to criticize oneself and is able to accept criticism depends to quite a considerable extent upon how one's upbringing has helped one to form appropriate pro-attitudes in this respect. Nevertheless, it does seem to me that as far as normal people are concerned—and however thin the distinction between normality and abnormality may be, it will not do to say that there is no such distinction at all—it is possible, in principle, for one to realize the inadequacy of one's existing attitudes and be willing to change them, however true it may, as a matter of fact, be that few people actually do question their attitudes. But a difficulty still remains. Changing an existing attitude, however undesirable one regards this attitude to be, is no easy task, and people show more or less capacity for the sustained effort that is necessary for success in this respect. Some people, we say, have more strength of character or will-power than others. How can people remodel their attitudes if they are lacking in the will-power that is necessary to do so?

Now I do not know that it has ever been shown that there is a necessary connection between a particular physiological and neurological constitution and a certain degree of what is called will-power, although it is likely that the extent to which one could exercise this power is restricted, within wide limits, by one's constitutional make-up. People who are constitutionally strong are perhaps capable of greater effort than people who are constitutionally weak. But there is no necessary connection between the two. In fact, some constitutionally weak people do show great tenacity in the field of their interest, but perhaps they are exceptional in some ways. In any case, we could hardly say that the strength of will that is necessary to make satisfactory moral choices through redirection of attitudes under ordinary circumstances is constitutionally lacking in normal people whether or not they actually exercise it. But some moral choices do call for great strength of will and courage which perhaps only people of a certain type of constitutional make-up are capable of. But we do not ordinarily blame people for not doing things that require great effort, courage, strength or sacrifice; and even if we do we should not, unless we are sure of the capabilities of the people concerned in these respects.

Thus psychology has indeed a lesson to teach us. It is not that we should cease to blame people altogether but that we must not judge different people in the same way for the same failures. We must take into account not only the pressure of existing circumstances but also the predominant circumstances in a man's life during those years when he was not yet capable of exercising independent judgment and when important habits and attitudes took shape. If we know of a man that he has had a bad upbringing, that he was helped very little or not at all in modifying his natural tendencies, that the circumstances of his early life were such as to cause much more frustration than fulfilment which is likely to give rise to a general feeling of resentment and so on, we should—and perhaps we do—make far greater allowances for his failures than for those of a man who was fortunate in these respects. But it does seem to me that people—people whom we would call normal, at any rate—do have the capacity to decide to do certain things which are not what their predominant tendencies and attitudes, that have hitherto been existing, are impelling them to do. That is to say, people are capable of changing the direction of their existing character in some ways (although perhaps not every time this is called for); that is what is implied in calling a man an agent or in saying that a man is capable of voluntary action. As it is only man amongst all created things that is capable of voluntary action perhaps it appears somewhat mysterious; and a mystery it is, in the sense that there is nothing in our experience in terms of which it could fully be explained.

There is another variety of determinism, that of psychoanalysis, which differs as a doctrine in some ways from ordinary psychological determinism. Some psycho-analysts believe that the character that we shall have as adults is fully determined by the experiences that we undergo during the first five years of our lives. During these years we are led to repress or completely banish from our conscious minds those impulses, desires and tendencies (felt naturally by all of us) which are not approved of by people amongst whom we live and against which pressure is brought to bear in the form of prohibitions and punishment. These impulses, etc., however still live with us as unconscious forces determining the shape of the activities that take place in our conscious minds. Further, some desires not socially disapproved of, like the desire to be loved, are sometimes frustrated as a result of the insensitivity of people who could fulfil it. A legitimate desire, if frustrated, creates a certain twist in our personalities that we do not even know of since it lives in our unconscious mind as a form of anti-social tendency.

Now the psycho-analytical concept of 'unconscious' differs from the same concept as ordinarily used, as in 'until that happened she was quite unconscious of the attachment she had for him'. By the use of the term 'unconscious' psycho-analysis means to convey much more than this that there is more in our personality than we know of at any one moment; or even that we remain quite unaware of some of our tendencies and attitudes that lend colour to our approach to things, unless something happens to force them on our attention. It says that we do not and cannot know of the basic forces that determine how we would think, feel and act because these forces have been driven out of the region of our consciousness by the special technique of repression and are accessible only by another special technique, namely psycho-analysis. The belief that we can control our motives and attitudes is an illusion, for we cannot even know what our important motives and attitudes are.

Even if the sweeping generalizations of this particular school of psycho-analysis are true, it would not completely rule out the use of moral praise and blame. It is possible for some people, at any rate, to be psycho-analysed very thoroughly—a process which brings to the fore forces which lie buried in the unconscious—and a psycho-analysed person is, theoretically at any rate, in a position to try to control the forces that have so long been controlling him.

But the generalizations of psycho-analysis are sweeping. The only adequate justification for postulating unconscious determining forces (in the psycho-analytical sense) is the presence in a person of behaviour difficulties of a compulsive type. So long as a person behaves normally and is able to vary his behaviour with changes in circumstances there is at least as much reason to think that the forces that are making him decide in one way rather than in another are accessible to a normal process of reflection and self-analysis, if such a process is resorted to, as to think that they are of an 'unconscious' nature. Now, although we do not know at first glance whether a particular piece of human behaviour represents a difficulty of a compulsive type, it is surely not impossible for us to find out, in most cases at any rate, whether a person behaves as he does out of some sort of compulsion that he is not aware of, when we have observed him behave in a number of situations. A compulsive behaviour-difficulty does bring with it traces of strain and anxiety, also it has little of that adaptability to circumstances which normal behaviour has. In any case, if we could not tell the difference we would never know whom to bring to the psycho-analyst for treatment and whom not. A psycho-analyst would no doubt reply that the mere fact that we do not think that a person ought to be psycho-analysed does not show that he is not acting under unconscious forces. I am not concerned to say that it does show this. It is likely that there are in all of us certain forces which determine some of our actions that need more than ordinary reflection and analysis for us to be aware of them. Not only so, even when these are brought to our notice we have a strong tendency to deny even to ourselves that they form a part of us. We are thus unconscious of these forces in a sense which is quite close to the psycho-analytical sense. What I am concerned to deny is that we must always act under such forces. On the contrary, I believe that we can come to know by ordinary processes of reflection some of the tendencies and motives that lead us to decide in one way rather than in another, although they may not be apparent to begin with. I do not even think that in a case of a conflict between tendencies that are at least potentially conscious and tendencies that are unconscious the unconscious tendencies must always win. Sometimes we find that we are being moved towards a certain direction by inner forces that baffle our understanding, but even though such forces have great driving power we do not necessarily yield. And when we do not, it is a part of our mental make-up belonging to the potentially conscious region that withholds the pressure of a compulsive force whose nature we do not quite understand. Of course, some people have more of an analytical bent of mind than others, and this one must have in order that one may delve into one's own subconscious and semi-conscious motives and attitudes and thereby gain an increasing understanding of one's own self. But I do not know whether this is fully determined by constitutional factors, i.e. whether we could say on the basis of our knowledge of a particular constitution that the man concerned is incapable of reflective self-analysis. In any case, it seems to me that one could be helped to a certain extent in this matter by suitable handling and guidance, provided one has the requisite degree of intelligence.

What I think psycho-analysis is justified in saying is that when we hold people—who behave in some undesirable way— responsible for their actions we are sometimes mistaken, not that we always are. We are sometimes mistaken, for it is possible and likely that unconscious motivation (i.e. beyond the immediate control of the individual concerned) is present in some instances of human behaviour which are not markedly abnormal and are therefore not obviously diagnosed as pathological. It is impossible from the very nature of the case to provide any criterion by which we could easily detect our mistakes in this respect. But I think that there is a rough commonsense way of guessing—this is applicable only when we have observed a person behave in a certain way on a number of occasions—whether a person is acting under forces of which he is not only unaware but which he is not even able to recognize as forming a part of his own self. This is not a very reliable guide, but it is not thoroughly unreliable either. In any case, the difference between the conscious and the unconscious mind is not as radical in normal human beings as psycho-analysis says—and this is compatible with a complete break between the two in pathological cases (or in so far as an instance of behaviour is an indication of a pathological condition)—for it is sometimes possible for us to recognize, without undergoing a process of psycho-analysis, that certain tendencies and attitudes are present in us which we not only did not know to be present but which we did not think could possibly be present in us until evidence for their presence is forcibly brought to our notice.

Now let us consider a theory which may be called cosmological determinism. Every event, says the cosmological determinist, must have a cause from which it follows necessarily. Human choice, being an event amongst events, must also have a cause; i.e. when a man chooses in a certain way, the possible alternatives being of a certain character, there must be a particular state of his mind from which it has followed necessarily, otherwise it remains a thing unexplained. Now it is a fact that an action proceeds from a certain state of the mind; an action could hardly be uncaused in the sense that it just happens without their being any history behind it of any kind whatsoever. But the point is, how rigid is the connection between a certain state of the mind and a particular action. And a theory is not a theory of determinism unless it advocates a rigid connection; that is to say, unless it says not only that a particular action has been preceded by a certain state of the mind but also that, given a certain state of the mind and the possible alternatives of choice, it can accurately be predicted what action will follow. But as a matter of fact, the connection between a given state of the mind and a particular action is not always as rigid as determinism would like to have it. Maurice Cranston has argued this point with great skill in his book *Freedom*. 'Imagine I have a friend who is parsimonious. If I said to him: "I'm sure you won't give a Christmas box at the club this year", he might take my words as an accusation of meanness, and promptly, in an attempt to disprove this allegation, hand a five-pound note to the porter at the club. Likewise a don may say to his best pupil: "You will get a first in the schools" and to his worst pupil: "You will get a fourth." The effect of the words on the very good pupil may be to give him too much confidence, cause him to relax in his preparation for the schools, and finally to take a second; the effect of the prediction on the very poor pupil may be to sting him to new efforts with the result that he pulls off a third.'[1]

If we consider the past mental history of the parsimonious friend and even his mental state at the moment of parting with the money which is possibly, partly at any rate, one of unwillingness to do so, we find that the action of handing over the money does not follow from either of these with any sort of necessity. The determinist would, of course, say in reply that the action does follow from this mental state of the parsimonious friend that he wishes to disprove the allegation of meanness. So it does, but the

[1] *Freedom*, p. 164.

fact that it does does nothing to undermine the possibility of genuine moral choice. It is only when the parsimonious friend is fully determined in his behaviour by his habit of parsimony that he is incapable of exercising any choice, not when he acts on the motive 'let me disprove that I am parsimonious' which does not follow necessarily from the habit of parsimony. When we say that we know a person to be parsimonious we mean that he is very sparing in expending money. The conclusion that we may arrive at deductively—on the occasion of the remark being made—from the knowledge that a man is parsimonious is that he will either ignore it or give only a small sum of money but not that he will give a comparatively large sum which it is strictly not necessary for him to spend. The deduction will be as follows:

> A parsimonious man will either not give any money at all or give as little as the circumstances permit, whenever the question of giving arises.
> This man is a parsimonious man.
> This man will either not give any money at all or give as little as the circumstances permit on this occasion.

As five pounds is a large sum of money to give as a Christmas box, our knowledge that a man is parsimonious could not possibly lead us to think that the man will give five pounds by any process that may be called 'necessary'. So long as it is allowed that human beings can have motives which are not just deductions from their past history, they can with justice be praised or blamed for their actions. When we say that a person is a moral agent we surely do not mean that he can act without motives, only that he retains the capacity of developing new motives if he wishes to, and not merely of acting on motives that he already finds in himself. But is he free to wish to do so or is one still being determined whether one wishes to develop new motives or merely follow the ones already present? If by saying 'one is still determined when one wishes to act on a motive that is opposed to the ones hitherto present in one' is simply meant that there is always a reason to be found when one wishes like this, then, of course, one is always determined. But this sort of determinism will not do the job for the determinist. Take, for instance, the case of the parsimonious friend. His action of handing over the money was determined (in the sense of being occasioned) by the remark 'I am sure that you will not give a Christmas box at the club this year'. The remark may be called the cause of his action in this sense that if the remark had not been made he would not have acted as he did. Now suppose that the same remark was made the next year. Is there any guarantee that the man will again hand over a five-pound note as he did before? It is doubtful whether he will. He might have seen through the remark by now, specially because the loss of those five pounds has probably caused him many an unhappy moment. Instead of thinking to himself 'let me disprove that I am parsimonious' he might think 'I am not going to be tricked by this remark this time', and consequently not give the money. Now suppose again that exactly the same remark was repeated on the third year. Is he going to avoid payment as he did the year before? Again it is doubtful. He might have felt very uneasy at having acted in a way which proves the accusation of parsimony commonly brought against him and he might hold that the repetition of the remark on the second year (giving him the impression that it was made to make him pay) was responsible for his not having paid. When he hears the remark for the third time he might say to himself 'I am not going to be tricked by this remark again', and hand over the money. Here the immediate cause of his action would be the same thought that made him act as he did on the previous year, but the same effect would not follow. Now it may be said that the thought 'I am not going to be tricked by this remark' actually stood for two different things on two different occasions. It meant on the first occasion 'I am not going to be tricked into paying', while on the second 'I am not going to be tricked into not paying'. But the determinist's case is still lost if the same remark can give rise to different thoughts on different occasions and there is no knowing which thought is going to be evoked on a certain occasion. Predictability is the touchstone of scientific determinism and, as Maurice Cranston shows, the issue of freedom in morals is the issue whether or not all human behaviour is predictable, in principle.

And I think that he succeeds in showing that it is impossible to predict some human behaviour, particularly creative behaviour, although we can sometimes predict with success how some people whom we know very well are going to act in a situation of a certain sort, particularly if we keep the prediction to ourselves. A moral action which is not fully covered by established habits may in a certain sense be called a creative act, for it represents an imaginative approach to a unique situation and a sensitive solution of what is essentially complex (i.e. not clear cut). However much we may know about a person and the circumstances under which he acts, we cannot tell beforehand how he is going to act, except when we have worked out the solution ourselves and our two solutions coincide. The determinist would no doubt reply that this is because we do not know enough. If we knew of everything that passed in the man's mind down to the point when he would just be ready to act we would also have known how he is going to act. This certainly is true. But the determinist is now saying no more than 'whatever is going to be, is going to be' and not that a certain action is going to be, for if we know all that there is to know down to the actual initiation of the action itself we also know the action that is going to be. But the point is, can we always tell what is going to be? And if we cannot, then we cannot hold on to determinism as the term would be understood in a scientific context. We can only accept it in the innocuous sense that every occurrence has certain precedents. Is it possible for us to know everything that is going to pass through a man's mind of which his action is only a natural outcome? To say that it is possible whether or not we actually do so is to assume that all this is somehow already set down. For if these are not set down and are still in the realm of possibility down to the moment when they do actually take place, then we can never know them before they have actually taken place, and to know this is to know not something that is going to be but something that already is.

In fact the formula 'whatever is going to be, is going to be' or 'whatever is, is' is all that cosmological determinism can with justification stand for, and it is quite compatible with the possibility of voluntary action which is what is presupposed in moral praise and blame. Now the formula 'whatever is, is' does express a necessity, a sort of necessity that we express when we say 'a thing done cannot be undone'. Because of this element of necessity the formula has also been expressed by 'whatever exists, exists of necessity'. But this latter formula might be taken to involve more than the necessity of an accomplished fact; it might be interpreted as, 'whatever comes to exist, must come to exist' and this suggests that the fact that is now accomplished was already *preordained*, or pre-formed. It suggests that whatever comes to exist can only do so by being pushed into existence by a definite set of conditions that lies behind, which in its turn is pushed into existence by something else further back and so on, so that all that is happening is happening according to a plan, as it were, which is already laid down in the very beginning of existence. This involves much more than what either of the tautologies 'whatever is, is' and 'whatever must be, must be' stand for, for it says 'whatever is, must be'. 'Whatever is, must be' is not a tautology nor is it unquestionably true as an empirical statement, for we have already noticed instances of human actions which do not fit in with this formula. Whatever is, must be, only if all the conditions that are actually involved in the coming into existence of a particular thing are already existing; but if we already know what these conditions are and that they are existing we know that the thing which is, is one that must be. That is to say, we have converted 'whatever is, must be' to 'whatever must be, must be'. And this is a tautology and as such acceptable without question. But it will not do the job that a cosmological determinist wants the formula 'whatever is, must be' to do.

Spinoza, who was a cosmological determinist, believed that all that happens in this world, including human actions, is pre-ordained and follows of necessity from nature considered as infinite and eternal which is another name for God. Belief in free choice and decision is then an illusion and judgments of praise and blame are without foundation. Believing as he did that human emotions follow the general laws of nature that are beyond human control, Spinoza thought that human failures should be looked upon as natural things like sunshine or grey sky, and not as things that can be either praised or blamed for being what they are. I believe that we are sometimes blamed for certain failures which it is not possible for us to avoid or even to choose to avoid, but Spinoza is saying much more than that. He is saying that we cannot in justice be blamed for anything we do, for whatever we do, we do by way of following nature that we must follow. This is a position which our common sense finds unacceptable, for there are instances where we have no reason whatsoever to doubt that we could have acted differently if we had chosen and that it is as much within our power to choose what we have not chosen as to choose what we have chosen. What we actually choose in such a case depends on what we set ourselves to choose, and it is in this power that we have of setting ourselves to choose a certain thing that the freedom of the moral agent lies. That we can set ourselves to choose in a certain way rather than in another either of which is within our power to choose, cannot be proved. It is something that has to be accepted, if it is accepted at all, on the evidence of those who have undergone the sort of experience that is involved in one's being a moral agent in the full sense of the term.

Do we then or do we not follow nature in choosing to act in one way rather than in another? It depends on what we mean by the term 'nature'. If by 'nature' we mean all that there has been, is, or will be, as Spinoza conceives nature to be by calling it infinite and eternal, then, of course, we could never escape nature whatever we may set ourselves to choose. For it includes all our actual or possible choice by definition. And when someone thinks of nature in this way—without beginning or end and yet existing as a totality in one's imagination—which seems to be rather a religious than a moral way of looking at things, it does seem to confer upon him an ability to accept calmly all that may happen, and to see human follies and failures in a wide perspective. And this perhaps makes him far less angered and upset at their presence than he would otherwise be. A religious attitude does not say that there is no difference between good and evil, or that nothing can be done to stop evil or bring about good, which would be the case if both good and evil are absolutely inevitable. But it does seem to enable a person to bear with equanimity, to some degree at any rate, the presence of evil when it has come to exist and to have a certain patience towards it as long as it must unavoidably exist, for he sees it as part of a much bigger something. To a person like this, whatever is going to happen is an integral part of what may be called 'reality' and this attitude of acceptance towards what is still not there in the ordinary sense makes what is already there somehow appear to be a part of what is past and as a result less provocative of resentment.

But as long as we are not talking from the religious point of view we do not include in our thoughts of nature whatever that will be when it will be and conceive of it as something that actually exists. Understood in this sense we do not inevitably follow our nature (which is a part of Nature infinite and eternal) in whatever we do, for sometimes we alter or remodel the nature that we already have. And so long as we do not include all that is going to happen in the future in our thought of the present, it does appear that we have the power to go against our nature. From this point of view, what is called one's 'nature' is not something that is eternally accomplished but something which may yet grow, and although this growth happens within certain wide limits, these limits do not preordain how a person would actually choose in every given situation (except perhaps a few). Understood merely as the doctrine—which is hardly a doctrine but may be a significant reminder in some ways—that every action that is performed must have a mental state which preceded it and not that the mental state that precedes the action in question can be the only state that could possibly have preceded it, cosmological determinism is true enough, but it is determinism only in a very inoffensive sense—in the sense that an action, particularly an action involving choice, does not suddenly appear out of nowhere but has a history behind it. But this sort of view cannot claim that we must act in some particular way or other.

I have so far tried to uphold the possibility, in principle, of genuine moral choice and the acceptability of judgments of praise and blame. But of all moral judgments, judgments of praise and blame are the most problematic in nature. Although we sometimes take it for granted that if we are justified in saying 'Y not Z was the duty of X' we are also justified in blaming X for not doing Y, this may not at all be the case. The judgment 'Y was the duty of X' may only put forward what was the most suitable act under a certain circumstance from the point of view of morality without at all implying that X in particular was theoretically able and practically in a position to do it. No doubt it appears contradictory to say that something can be somebody's duty if the person concerned is not able to do it. That is when we use the term 'duty' to mean 'personally obliged to do'. It must be admitted that most often we do use 'duty' in this way. And when we do so we also blame the person concerned for not doing what is his duty. But sometimes it happens that we do want to say that some other act than the one done by somebody is morally the most suitable act under the circumstances, although we find that we cannot in justice hold the person responsible and therefore blameworthy for not having done it. The term 'duty' not only means 'personally obliged to do', it also means 'the most suitable act under the circumstances'. But having used the word in this wide sense we often lapse into the habit of thinking that duty must mean 'personally obliged to do', and as we do so we blame a person we should not in justice blame. When we talk about general obligation we conceive human nature to be of a certain kind. This is the kind which we suppose belong to one whom we would call a normal human being, i.e. a person who is not deficient in his abilities or diseased in their functioning or again who is not lacking in opportunities of developing himself or of social adjustment to a degree that is prejudicial to one's becoming a moral agent. And these we judge by comparing different people with one another even though we can have only more or less tenable opinions in such matters and not knowledge. When we use the word 'duty' in its narrower sense we also express our belief that X is a normal human being in the morally relevant sense. But we do not always take care to find out if this really is the case, as we should. For people's inabilities which may be called 'natural' in the sense that they make a genuine moral choice of a certain kind impossible are not always apparent. And we might find on closer considerations that although a particular act is the most suitable in a certain circumstance, and although it is not impossible for normal people to do it, the person actually involved could not be expected to do it because of some inability or other over which he has no control. Then we would be justified in saying 'Y was the duty of X' only in the sense that Y was the most suitable act which he, if he was not suffering from some inability that he cannot be expected to control, would have been obliged to do. And this makes it clear that X cannot be blamed for not doing what was his duty in this wider sense. A judgment of duty in this wider sense is a judgment on something that is of value considered on its own, a judgment that blames is a judgment on somebody or other in particular who may or may not be able to achieve what is of value because of certain factors that are beyond his control. But if we are not always justified in assuming that a person, in particular, is able to do his duty neither are we justified in assuming that he is not so able; and we should have good reasons in favour of thinking that he is not able to, if we are going to think that he is not. A judgment of blame has then only a provisional validity and is subject to correction in the light of any further evidence that may be forthcoming, although, even after such correction, we may continue to believe that the act, for the failure to do which the man was being blamed, is, considered by itself, morally most suitable to the situation.

It is not only that a judgment of blame has only a provisional validity; the concept of 'blame' is a concept in terms of which we hold people more or less responsible for their failures. We might find that although a particular person is not inherently incapable of doing the act which is suitable to the situation the doing of it might need a considerable amount of effort or sacrifice on the part of the agent. If a case of moral failure is a case like this, we do not feel disposed to hold the agent fully responsible for his failure. For when we hold a person fully responsible for doing what he, in a certain sense, should not have done, we feel disgust at his conduct. But we do not feel disgust for every moral failure for which an agent is, in some ways, responsible. For we realize that some circumstances are such that it is relatively easy to do what one ought to do while others offer a great deal of temptation to a moral agent to do what he should not do. Now there may not, theoretically speaking, be any reason why one must give way to a certain temptation; but considering that human beings are not angels, whose characters are conceived in such a way that they can only do what is good and not what is evil, we feel that it is in some sense natural for one to give way to temptation if the temptation is strong. This is why we do not show contempt or disgust for failures that are not easily avoidable as we may do for failures which can be avoided relatively easily. It is obvious that there is no set criterion by which one could in every case automatically find out what failures are easily avoidable and what are not, but this does not mean that there is no difference between the two or that it is impossible from the very nature of the case to find out which is which. It only shows that there can be no ready-made judgments of praise or blame, and that every single case ought to be thought out on its own merit. Just as our particular judgments of duty ought to be based on considerations of specific situations in which actions take place, so also our particular judgments of blame ought to be based on the specific capabilities of the agent concerned as well as the circumstances that strongly influence him. Our particular judgments of duty and blame are then not deductions from self-evident premises but they involve certain self-evident notions of value which give a perspective to such particular judgments.

Most of what we have said about blame applies also to praise. Just as we do not, or should not, blame all people equally for the same failures we do not praise them equally for the same success either. If people have superior capabilities or are fortunate in the circumstances of life, some ways of behaving required by the moral point of view come relatively easily to them. Others who start at a disadvantage in some ways may have to exert great pressure on themselves for the same success. We are inclined to praise the latter people more than we praise the former, for obviously the latter type of action represents more in terms of positive achievement, although, as Kant says, anyone who does whatever his duty in preference to what is not is thereby worthy of respect. Again the same person is praised more for doing a particular duty temptation against which is strong than for one which gives him positive pleasure, although the fact that it gives him pleasure does not detract from the value that the doing of one's duty has. But we do not always praise people for doing their duties as we usually incline to blame all normal people for failing to do something that is their duty. And the reason for this seems to be this.

In every society certain ways of behaviour are generally established and they become, through various processes of social conditioning, a part of the habitual equipment that the members of the society in general have. People are not generally praised for doing those duties that are habitually done in a society, for to single out anyone for praise is to attribute to him personal credit and we do not think that anyone deserves personal credit for doing what is habitually done by most—although the fact that something is done habitually does not detract from the value that an action has as the doing of a duty.

Judgments of praise like judgments of blame are problematic, for we do not know for certain whether the doing of a duty by a certain man represents a personal achievement. But such judgments, although problematic, may be more or less well-grounded and here I have tried to expound the considerations on which they are, or ought to be, grounded. 'Praise' and 'blame' are concepts by means of which we ascribe more or less credit or discredit to people for doing what they do or for not doing what they do not do.

Index